The Art of
Joyce's Syntax
in *Ulysses*

The Art of
Joyce's Syntax
in *Ulysses*

by
Roy K. Gottfried

The University of Georgia Press
Athens

Copyright © 1980 by the University of Georgia Press
Athens 30602

Set in 11 on 14 point Caledonia type
Printed in the United States of America

Library of Congress Cataloging in Publication Data

Gottfried, Roy K
   The art of Joyce's syntax in *Ulysses*.
   Bibliography.
   Includes index.
    1. Joyce, James, 1882–1941. Ulysses. 2. Joyce,
James, 1882–1941—Style. I. Title.
PR6019.O9U6532   823'.9'12   79–10294
ISBN 0–8203–0478–6

To Oliver

"You have been seeking the *mot juste?*" I asked.
"No," said Joyce. "I have the words already. What
I am seeking is the perfect order of the words in the
sentence. There is an order in every way appropriate."
Frank Budgen, *The Making of Ulysses*

Contents

Acknowledgements

A book on Joyce, no matter how limited its scope and its contribution, cannot fully discharge its debts; those professional are too broad, those personal, too deep. For the former, the bibliography must inadequately serve; for the latter, the following: to Charles Feidelson, for his patience with an embryonic idea and a recalcitrant dissertation; to Martin Price for early words of encouragement; to Robert Scholes for constant help and interest. Bernie Benstock and David Hayman both read the manuscript at various stages with care and concern; their comments and criticism are most appreciated. The dedication acknowledges a debt, short standing but indelible, something more than a legal fiction.

The third part of grammar is Syntax, which shows the agreement and right disposition of words in a sentence. A sentence is an assemblage of words, expressed in proper order, and concurring to make a complete sense.

Lindley Murray, *English Grammar*

He then recollected the morning littered bed etcetera and the book about Ruby with met him pike hoses in it which must have fell down sufficiently appropriately beside the domestic chamberpot with apologies to Lindley Murray.   *Ulysses*

1 Joycean Syntax as Appropriate Order

As a fatigued and drunken Stephen listens to Bloom at the cabman's shelter, "he could hear, of course, all kinds of words changing colour like those crabs about Ringsend in the morning, burrowing quickly into all colours of different sorts of the same sand where they had a home somewhere beneath or seemed to."[1] The reader of *Ulysses* has a similar if not quite synaesthetic response to the language of the novel: even in these few sentences he sees words change, not color, but position and place. Prepositional phrases are repeatedly strung together ("about Ringsend in the morning"; "of different sorts of the same sand") while adverbs alternate with prepositions: "they had a home somewhere beneath." The sentence shifts ground abruptly, breaking off with a verb phrase that seems to undo the simile constructed: "like crabs . . . or seemed to." Parts of speech burrow like those crabs throughout the syntax of this sentence, and their alteration is a most prominent feature.

1

Such movement and rearrangement of parts are the most noticeable features of any sentence in the large novel. Rhythm, rhyme, and sound patterns are also important features, as all contribute to texture and sense, but the syntactic changes are the most striking. The parts of speech which burrow through the syntax of the sentence are perhaps less like crabs than like Hamlet's "enginers," sappers actually undermining the order of the sentence with appropriately explosive results. Recognizable grammatical elements are scrambled in startling ways. "Mr Best entered, tall, young, mild, light. He bore in his hand with grace a notebook, new, large, clean, bright" (186). Beyond the poetics of rhythm and rhyme in this sentence, there is a strategy; by moving the object, *notebook*, to the end of the predicate, thus putting the prepositional phrases in between and out of the way, a long string of adjectives can be built. That string would hardly have room had normal order been followed; rearrangement of syntax makes some very useful breeches.

The results of this engineering are prevalent throughout the text, and every part of speech can be the means for a new explosive arrangement. The process of displacement gives concrete status to the nouns as grammatical objects in this sentence: "All watched awhile through their windows caps and hats lifted by passers" (88); while compression of verbs can make for a comic effect in this: "plunging his knife into her until it just struck him that" (642). Displacement gives an air of anticipation to every sentence, and this following adverb is made possible by a proleptic glance at the description of its object: "[he] moved slowly frogwise his green legs in the . . . water" (21).

As every part of speech is a means for disordering and

re-ordering, it is no surprise to find a sentence completely
undermined, a reversed and razed image of normal order:
"From drains, clefts, cesspools, middens arise on all sides
stagnant fumes" (433).

The features of syntactic displacement are observable in
the language of every chapter. In a book of "eighteen different points of view and . . . as many styles," as Joyce
wrote to Harriet Shaw Weaver,[2] these features of manipulation might be the common denominator of all the chapters and characters. The example which began this chapter
was the narrator of "Eumaeus." Stephen's monologue is
certainly unmistakable and different. "Me sits there with
his augur's rod of ash, in borrowed sandals, by day beside
a livid sea, unbeheld, in violet night walking beneath a
reign of uncouth stars" (48). Such touches as the archaic
and inverted "rod of ash" and the pathetic fallacy "uncouth stars" are its chief marks of recognition. Yet his
monologue is no less noticeable for its changes: phrases
intrude here in different positions as each refers backward
and forward. The adjective *unbeheld* in the center refers
back to the ungrammatical *me,* subject of the sentence;
the phrase "by day" is adverbial and modifies the verb *sit.*
The prepositional phrase "in borrowed sandals" refers back
to the subject, but "in violet night" refers to the participle
that follows it, *walking.* In turn, that participle modifies
the subject at the beginning of the sentence. Throughout
even this self-consciously poetic sentence there is the careful transformation of syntax into a shifting and a striking
new form.

Bloom's monologue, so characteristic of him and so different from Stephen's, also evidences these features. "The
far east. Lovely spot it must be: the garden of the world,

3

big lazy leaves to float about on, cactuses, flowery meads, snaky lianas they call them" (71). Here what seems to be a series of nouns is interposed between two predicates, "leaves to float on" and "lianas they call them." Bloom depicts Molly thus: "Looking at me, the sheet up to her eyes, Spanish, smelling herself" (84). Each phrase describes his wife, but each has a different grammatical construction. Long sentences become entangled as they are ordered in Bloom's mind: "Windy night that was I went to fetch her there was that lodge meeting on about those lottery tickets after Goodwin's concert" (156). The *there* is not an adverb modifying *fetch* but rather a pronoun, subject of the sentence "there was that lodge meeting." *After* refers not to the time of that meeting but rather refers all the way back to when Bloom "went to fetch"; it skips over the lodge and the lottery, the secrets of Bloom's life. Prepositions brought together collide: "meeting on about."

The omniscient narrator, or authorial voice, is an entity of some question in the polyphonic narrative of *Ulysses*. Yet all his voices are characterized consistently by the unique configuration of syntax. Bloom's "eyes sought answer from the river and saw a rowboat rock at anchor on the treacly swells lazily its plastered board" (153): the placing of the two prepositional phrases gives a suggestion that the verb *rock* is intransitive ("he saw a rowboat rock"); yet the insertion of the noun phrase at the end makes the verb transitive and thrusts back into the sentence with the requirements of grammar (and it also reveals the presence of the artist's hand in ordering). Similarly, the delay caused by the intrusion of various phrases in this sentence suggests the control of the narrative voice: "Moving through the air high spars of a threemaster, her sails brailed up on

4

the crosstrees, homing, upstream, silently moving, a silent ship" (51). Even a declarative sentence of encyclopaedic cataloguing demonstrates a change in syntactic order: "From Six Mile Point, Flathouse, Nine Mile Stone follow the footpeople with knotty sticks, salmongaffs, lassos" (572).

Distinguishing in the text between character's monologue and just such an "authorial" voice is a continual problem in the interpretation of *Ulysses*. Much is to be gained by determining the transfer of points of view; yet in order to do so, one must first recognize the basic elements that make them so similar and hard to distinguish from one another. As the above examples illustrate, all parts of the text share common characteristics at the level of syntax. The disorder and rearranging, features obtaining regardless of speaker, are precisely what unites character and narrator and creates a common ground between them. The jumbled order of a sentence brings the internal and external of the novel into tangency. In pushing the prepositional phrase "to the yard" to the end of the following sentence, away from the verb it modifies, Joyce creates an opening in the line that allows for the change in perspective and gives him the opportunity to combine two viewpoints. (It also, incidentally, gives the phrase a sly ambiguity.) "A man and ready he drained his glass to the lees and walked, to men too they [goddesses] gave themselves, manly conscious, lay with men lovers, a youth enjoyed her, to the yard" (176–77). The last phrase, prepositional, belongs to the narrator's third person "he . . . walked"; Bloom's thoughts about the sex lives of goddesses intervene in the gap. The reordered syntax of *Ulysses* enables both character and narrator to be united: it is the common area of their respective presences

5

in the text. Moreover, the syntax is the means by which they can also be distinguished.

As might be apparent from the previous cursory examples, there is something unique, fundamental, and pervasive about the syntax of *Ulysses*. It is unlike that of Joyce's earlier works, and in some measure unlike that of his last. The very opening of the novel presents a language clearly operating with its own sense of linguistic order in which adverbs and adjectives share prominence with the subject of the sentence—even with, as in this case, a character: "Stately, plump Buck Mulligan"; "Halted, he peered"; "Solemnly, he came." Such particularities of a changed syntactic order can be observed in all forms of language within the text.

The novel's recreation of spoken forms, its oral dimension, is informed by the unique character of its syntax. Sentences such as "snails out of the ground the French eat" (174), or "sun's heat it is" (175), which have been called an "Irish type of sentence,"[3] display the propensity for altering normal order. A direct object and a predicate nominative, respectively, are replaced, pushed to the opening of the sentence, and illustrate the features of Joyce's manipulated syntax.

Much as with the recreation of oral speech, so too the novel's recreation of written language illustrates the features of syntactic manipulation. A boldface headline in "Aeolus" gives prominence to a prepositional phrase, then follows it with a pronoun: "WITH UNFEIGNED REGRET IT IS WE ANNOUNCE . . ." (118).

Joyce's mode of composition, his brooding over the text, adding to it and aggrandizing it, as Litz's and more recent studies have shown,[4] produces some noteworthy changes

6

in the language. Here are two parts at different stages of writing, first an early typescript and second the final text in the novel (intermediate stages of composition have been suppressed).

> —*As it were, in the peerless panorama of bosky grove and undulating plain and luscious pastureland, steeped in the translucent glow of our mild Irish twilight . . .*
>
>   .   .   .
>
> —*As 'twere, in the peerless panorama of Ireland's portfolio, unmatched, despite their wellpraised prototypes in other vaunted prized regions, for very beauty, of bosky grove and undulating plain and luscious pastureland of vernal green, steeped in the transcendent translucent glow of our mild mysterious Irish twilight . . .* (125)

The changes are all made with the obvious intent of inflating the text—the chapter is "Aeolus," its art windy rhetoric—"peerless panorama of Ireland's portfolio." Yet the changes result in a very clear syntactic manipulation. Prepositions are separated from their antecedents: "portfolio . . . of," "unmatched . . . for"; adjectives separated from their nouns: *unmatched* from *panorama, steeped* from any number of possibilities. It could hardly be argued that Joyce's mode of composition is the result of his ordering of syntax; but it is probably not the cause either: the early text also demonstrates the manipulation. (For example, it already separates *panorama* from *steeped* and thus possibly explains the development of the later text.) Even in its composition, one finds Joyce's language ordered and disordered.

Sentences are opened to syntactic displacement and ag-

7

grandizement in the final stage of the printed text itself. On one page in "Wandering Rocks" there is the following simple sentence: "Mr Kernan, pleased with the order he had booked, walked boldly along James's street." One page later a mutation of this appears in all the newness of its altered syntax: "From the sundial towards James's Gate walked Mr Kernan pleased with the order he had booked for Pulbrook Robertson boldly along James's Street, past Shackleton's offices" (239). Starting with a prepositional phrase—the place, after all, Kernan starts from—the sentence inverts the order of subject and verb; then goes through an adjective phrase describing Kernan as pleased and an adverb describing the way he walked; and finally ends with two other prepositional phrases.

This manipulation of sentence parts, this refashioning of syntactic order, are the essential qualities of the Joycean sentence. Each and every sentence in the large novel is, in fact, a potential illustration of these features. Although a description of each sentence would be a difficult, almost impossible task, and several works address themselves to such a catalogue,[5] it is not the weight of the evidence that is discouraging (whenever was magnitude an obstacle to Joyce's readers?); the problem lies rather in the fact that any listing of sentences would merely enumerate incidences and accumulate statistics. The noticeable quality of every Joycean sentence suggests something beyond examples of original and creative language. *Ulysses* abounds in such sentences as "Waiting always for a word of help his hand moved faithfully the unsteady symbols" (28), and each sentence is subject to an artistic process which not only achieves the striking originality which is any particular example but which also, given the consistency of the

8

disordering, suggests more than the sentence itself. That quality of something beyond mere lexical engineering or accumulated statistic is worthy of consideration. Joyce wrote too carefully and conscientiously not to give any thought to the effect of each part; he risked the publication of *Dubliners* to preserve the integrity of his own choice. In a long exchange with Grant Richards over, among other issues, the word *bloody* in several stories, Joyce showed not only his pride in art but also his sense of that art's effect: "The word, the exact expression I have used ['He'd bloody well put his teeth down his throat,' from 'A Boarding House'], in my opinion the one expression in the English language which can create on the reader the effect which I wish to create."[6] What is true of a word in *Dubliners* can hardly be less true of the words in *Ulysses;* an episode recounted by Frank Budgen makes Joyce's awareness of his artistic choice abundantly clear: "'You have been seeking the *mot juste?*' (Budgen asked). 'No,' said Joyce. 'I have the words already. What I am seeking is the perfect order of the words in the sentence. There is an order in every way appropriate.'"[7] That appropriate order is clearly the order of syntax readapted so as to be appropriate to Joyce. It is more than shining creativity; it has a studied purpose and effect. An exploration of the syntax of *Ulysses* without the restrictions of statistics has the flexibility and the lattitude to explore what is effective and appropriate.

The intentional twists and turns of syntax, which create all the transformed constructions, are illustrative of certain characteristics of the Joycean sentence: a freedom within bounds, an extension of certain expected patterns of syntax to the limit of their rules, but not beyond. Joyce's language has a two-sided effect, one which explodes language

9

into new forms while still relying on the normal, expected order to render the new creation sensible.[8] The language is characterized by a tacit acceptance of the ordering rules of syntax while using those same rules to twist sentences into new images. Joyce makes his own "appropriate" way, as he says, "with apologies to Lindley Murray." Yet while the Dedalian craftsman beats the syntactic connections between his words to airy thinness, those connections remain strong and supplely effective. In every sentence, shifting series of phrases form agile connections in the language, thin but tenacious threads of meaning spun by the syntax and pulled by the artful repositioning. For Joyce, style was a matter of proper words in improper places: each sentence is pulled between the order of syntax and the freedom of newly created forms.

While sentences range in degree from order to openness, there is present within each sentence the sense of order which is the purpose of syntax. In the connections of proper form there is the suggestion of control and limit. Participles interspersed with active verbs fix precisely the movement of this sentence: "He fitted the book roughly into his inner pocket and, stubbing his toes against the broken commode, hurried out towards the smell, stepping hastily down the stairs with a flurried stork's legs" (65).

The alternation of phrasing and diction give the following paragraph a vibrancy oscillating between the poles of appropriate creativity and proper order. Aided by alliteration, in a chapter whose "art" is music, this is a syntactic theme played with variations. "Miss Kennedy sauntered sadly from bright light, twining a loose hair behind an ear. Sauntering sadly, gold no more, she twisted twined a hair. Sadly she twined in sauntering gold hair behind a curving ear" (258). Words appear in different forms, moving from verb to participle and back: *twining* changes to *twined* while *sauntered* changes to *sauntering*. The same adverb changes its referent: "sauntered sadly . . . sadly she twined." The participial phrase in each sentence appears in a different position: at end, beginning, and middle, respectively. The loose interplay of words and the alternation of parts are ultimately held in order by the form of syntax and yield a rhythmic tension of opposition.

The result of such creative disordering within syntactic structure is a motion of changing parts, and this can yield such sentences, grammatically correct but misleadingly meandering, as "It will (the air) do you good, Bloom said, meaning also the walk, in a moment" (660). Yet the disordering can also result in the freedom of artistic variety. "He foresaw his pale body reclined in it at full, naked, in a womb of warmth, oiled by scented melting soap, softly laved" (86). The sentence alternates prepositional phrases referring to the bathtub—"in it," "in a womb of warmth"—with adjectives referring to the object of the sentence, the body—"naked," "reclined," "oiled by," "softly laved."[9] The result is a moving lexical surface, fraught with the pull of order and disorder, proper form and appropriate, creative form.

The reason for Joyce's abuse within use of syntax lies chiefly in the fact that he wants both to give and to take. For all his anomalous creations of language, he needs the normal order of syntax not only to show off these creations to advantage, but also to render them understandable; as Lindley Murray claims, it is order that makes "a complete sense." Joyce draws attention to syntactic rules in one sentence in order to defy them in the next. The language of

Ulysses is a freedom within bounds, a freedom which takes its definition, as all freedoms do, from the order it makes free with. It relies on the limits of order to give it its creative opportunities.[10] *Ulysses* is a balance of formal experimentation with existing orders (forms of the novel, forms of sentences); and for all its being a supposed training ground for *Finnegans Wake*,[11] it distinguishes itself clearly, and in nothing more clearly than in its language. Normal syntax is there, a pattern which contains the vibrant language of the novel, just as a map of Dublin's streets would contain the voyages of an epic hero.

This two-sided attitude was possible because Joyce instinctively and actively recognized the paradoxical nature of language. Conscious of words even from his youth, a teacher of English and a speaker of three foreign tongues, he sensed two essential concurrent features of language. One is the very determined and fixed aspect dictated by the patterns of syntax. A sentence with the subject in the third person singular must, if it is to be understood, have the verb in the appropriate person; if that verb is transitive, the rules require that it be accompanied by a direct object, and so on until the closing period, when presumably all the requirements are met. The immediate effect of syntax is evident especially to one who tries to speak a foreign language: sentences move, indeed unroll themselves until they reach their end. This movement is language's second feature, closely aligned with and actually inseparable from the first; sentences move around, changing directions in a shifting looseness while they complete and in order to complete the requirements of syntax. While fixed, the sentences are free; while loose, they are constrained.

Such a contention also suggests that the defining terms

of Joyce's linguistic creativity are closely related, indeed interdependent. Each term takes its presence and meaning from the other, and both are necessary to describe Joyce's art. In the rhythmic example from "Sirens," cited earlier, it was evident that the characteristic license and order of the sentences were relative, that one sentence was defined by the text: "Miss Kennedy sauntered sadly from bright light, twining a loose hair behind an ear. Sauntering sadly, gold no more, she twisted twined a hair" (258).

Joyce's repatterning is present throughout the text: it consists of his twisting and reshaping of syntax according to his own sense of what is appropriate order. Thus he constantly establishes the general features of his disordering and repatterning within the span of any several sentences encountered. Take as a most obvious example the opening of the novel, where the reader is first exposed to the language of *Ulysses:* "Stephen suffered him to pull out and hold up on show by its corner a dirty crumpled handkerchief" (4). The two infinitive phrases are followed not by their object, nor by one prepositional phrase ("on show"), but by two, by way of increasing grammatic anticipation and finally resolving it. This so evident syntactic manipulation is Joyce's creative deviation from what one would consider normal syntactic form.

Yet that deviation in the face of normal order becomes, in its own turn, a standard or basis—if one will, a norm— for further experimentation and creative disruption by Joyce.[12] All of the language of his text is at one and the same time an order and a disorder in scales various to each other: having created his own deviations, Joyce uses them as a new order from which to work further transformations.

Such interdependence is possible because Joyce is never

absolutist, but ever careful to balance and offset any series of options, to keep them open, in flux, paradoxical, and poised. Similarly, the terms of order and appropriate disorder used here to describe what is so characteristic of Joyce's syntax are not absolute. Rather, interdependent as they are, they take their meaning in contrast to and in context with one another. Like Bloom and Molly in bed, their positions are determined "relatively to themselves and to each other" (737). The terms indicate the range of possibilities in both the deviations and the normative constructions; being interrelated and offset, they emphasize the different potentials of a language always twisted and refashioned.

> Richie, admiring, descanted on that man's glorious voice. He remembered one night long ago. Never forget that night. Si sang *'Twas rank and fame:* in Ned Lambert's 'twas. Good God he never heard in all his life a note like that he never did *then false one we had better part* so clear so God he never heard *since love lives not* a clinking voice ask Lambert he can tell you too.
>
> Goulding, a flush struggling in his pale, told Mr Bloom, face of the night, Si in Ned Lambert's, Dedalus' house, sang *'Twas rank and fame.*
>
> He, Mr Bloom, listened while he, Richie Goulding, told him, Mr Bloom of the night he, Richie, heard him, Si Dedalus, sing *'Twas rank and fame* in his, Ned Lambert's house. (276–77)

Here, in the span of three paragraphs whose subjects are nearly identical, the relativity of Joyce's linguistic poles is evident. The first paragraph approximates a normal order of syntax: "He remembered"; "in Ned Lambert's 'twas"; "Good God he never heard." The sentences are

14

nearly complete grammatical forms and are clearly ordered. The last phrases are somewhat abrupt, as the entire paragraph is clearly manipulated to render the immediacy of spoken language and the interruption of song in the next room.

The second paragraph blends the phrases of music with those of narrative, by making the echoes of the song grammatically part of the sentences: "Goulding, a flush"; "Bloom, face." The two clauses, "Goulding told," "Si Dedalus . . . sang," are set loose, not subordinated or joined. The effect of the manipulation of song and syntax—while in the service of the theme and technique of the chapter—provides a loosened surface which is rich with intonation, rhythm, and suggestiveness. By opening up the syntax, the potentials for construction and the possibilities for meaning are increased.

The third paragraph insists on an order of language as studied and maniacal as the language in a grammar book. Every pronoun as subject and object is listed, with the referents additionally supplied. The effect is to stress the rules of grammar, to insist on the order and system inherent in language which the preceding paragraphs manipulate to such purpose.

The three paragraphs descend, on the page and in some scale, down to a very tightened order of language which Joyce can exploit. The first paragraph might even be called a norm or average for Joyce: it is manipulated to render allusions as well as thoughts and conversations, and is grammatically clear but with gaps that open up the syntax. The middle paragraph takes language further, untying syntax into parataxis, suppressing grammatical connections, taking language towards all possible and appropriate variations. That paragraph illustrates the freedom of language and the openness of meaning; but clearly its freedom is constituted in relation to the other paragraphs around it and to the language of the novel. It is a freedom not absolute but relative, just as the control of the third paragraph is tightened and ordered in relation to that freedom.

The definition of these principles is made additionally relative by their context within the novel, where they appear and what they stress. As mentioned earlier, the styles that vary from chapter to chapter ultimately have their common denominator in the language being manipulated, but the terms of that manipulation are similarly open to adaptability and variety.

The result of the syntactic relativity is to yield both variety and order, freedom and fixity. Every deviation from normal syntactic order opens up increasingly the vast potentials that are in language. A sentence such as the following can only be a product of a language potentially open to variety: "[He] heard warm running sunlight and in the air behind him friendly words" (10). The rhythmic variety is achieved by the displacing of the prepositional phrase. There is here a similarity between Joyce's sentence and a line of Hopkins's "The Windhover": "in his riding / Of the rolling level underneath him steady air." Chronology does little to support a sense of indebtedness: Stephen could not have read Hopkins in 1904, and if Joyce later did, the fact is not known. Yet the similarity has its cause deeper than borrowings. In both writers there is a sense of stress caused by the order of language and the variety possible in playing off that order. Hopkins's "sprung rhythm" of instress is achieved by altering words from their expected metrical order. Joyce's appropriate language is made up of a release of words from the bonds of their normal syntactic order. In both men, there is the recognition of an existing order, and the tension which results in the opening up of that order to new forms and possibilities.

The language of *Ulysses* can be seen as using the characteristics of a syntax both open and closed to a particular purpose, setting them up against each other in a subtle tension. The various sentences described above stress the two factors clearly: they have a grammatical comprehension achieved by and within the prescribed freedom of the sentence parts. It is the free motion of the sentences which carries the stream of language along (as well as the "stream of consciousness" and even the narrative itself); it is the order of syntax which restrains and banks its course.

And indeed such channelled expression may be the only possible kind. There is a point at which, without order, thought and communication can no longer exist. Nietzsche appears only in some of Joyce's short-lived youthful fury and some jokes in *Ulysses*, but he expresses the necessity of order in language and thought in a way quite close to Joyce's silent assent and artful maneuvering: "Wir hören auf zu denken, wenn wir es nicht in dem sprachlichen Zwange tun wollen. . . . Das vernünftige Denken ist ein Interpretieren nach einem Schema."[13] ("We cease to think when we do not wish to think in linguistic constraints. Logical thinking is an exposition according to a pattern.") This is an admission of the need for a certain restriction ("Zwang") to make thought and communication possible. There is as well an expression of intent, even conscious desire, to work within those restrictions—*wollen*. Concomitant with this willingness there is a recognition of a freedom of interpretation and a variety possible within that system. These terms speak to the dual nature of the Joycean sentence. A freedom of movement and an awareness of the need for systems which bind and confine, these are characteristics of Joyce's life no less than of his life's work of art.

Joyce is the exile who left Dublin only to see it more clearly. There can hardly be a freedom of the *non serviam,* if there is no established religion to serve; nor is free thought (of which Stephen considers himself the "horrible example") possible without a dogma. Joyce's brother Stanislaus remarked astutely: "The interest that my brother always retained in the philosophy of the Catholic Church sprang from the fact that he considered Catholic philosophy to be the most coherent attempt to establish . . . an intellectual and material stability. In his own case, however, freedom was a necessity: it was the guiding theme of his life. He accepted its gifts and its perils as he accepted his own personality, as he accepted the life that produced him."[14] As in God's universe in *Paradise Lost,* the order is set to give man his choice: he is thus free, to choose and to fall; or, like the artist Dedalus, free to choose, to fly, and to fall. A freedom within bounds, a chaos amid order, this is the discord out of which Joyce makes the concord of the novel. There is the overall order of hours, places, organs, arts—the schemes Joyce gave to Linati and Gilbert—which seem inadequate to the book's myriad details and minute complexity; and in their inadequacy lies some measure of their usefulness, for without the original plan, the order, the pattern, no such cornucopia could be possible.[15] Joyce's was a mind which acquiesced to pattern, a mind medieval or Catholic, or both; plans and systems were not uncongenial to it. It needed the pattern to have the whole, to test the limits which it would then go up to, fill to the brim. The *Odyssey* itself may be a poor guide to the novel, but for Joyce it was the skeleton on which he could flesh out his art. A medieval Catholic mind had many prescribed plans, yet from such plans come the limitlessness of the *Divine Comedy* or the Cathedral of Chartres.

At the heart of Joyce's creativity lies the enigma that he must have limits in order to transgress them, set up schemes only to undo them. The order he makes for himself must be appropriated as well as appropriate; he must use all forms so as to create his own art. Order defines the limits to which he must go. He accumulates specific details about particular places and persons in Dublin to render the most cosmic perspective in which those very details lose meaning; conversely, he follows the outlines of a universal myth in order to render the most precise account of an event in a certain place and time. Joyce must use and master all the techniques of the nineteenth century artist to be the most original of the twentieth: he masters naturalism in order to turn his book towards symbolism. Paradoxes abound in *Ulysses* because of the particular nature of Joyce's creativity: the novel is pan- and myopic, specific and general, ordered and chaotic. At the base of all this lies the paradox of every created sentence of *Ulysses*, the striking newness of its language transformed through an awareness of the order it manipulates.

In a letter to his brother in 1905 Joyce says of himself, "The struggle against conventions in which I am at present involved was not entered into by me so much as a protest against these conventions as with the intention of living in conformity with my moral nature."[16] That moral nature was certainly a difficult and contradictory one, the few

19

times it displayed itself directly, yet Joyce recognizes that his is a nature which does not exist merely to flay conventions for the sake of flaying, but a nature profoundly concerned with finding its own way amid and among them.

Joyce the model student, the young artist, lived within system and order. Synge saw the young man as "obsessed by rules"; and even his lonely but vast reading at night in Paris libraries showed a desire for "formalism."[17] His Jesuit school training was planned centuries before, and Joyce followed it well. Jesuit teaching may not have given him a respect for religion, but it did teach him "the order of words" and a strong sense of syntax and grammar.[18]

One classroom exercise at Belvedere was a translation of an ode of Horace. The ten-year-old Joyce was careful to locate the correct parts of his translation in a most effective way. The Latin reads: "Fies nobilium tu quoque fontium, / me dicente cavis impositam ilicem / saxis, unde loquaces / lymphae desiliunt tuae" (3. 13). Joyce translated: "be of the noble founts! I sing / The oak tree o'er thine echoing / Crags, the waters murmuring." While heralding the postured formality of his own poetry, this piece of juvenilia is quite creative in its correctness: separating the adjective from its noun by means of the line break, Joyce makes it enact the form of a cliff. This simple exercise evidences a sensitivity for the expressive character and the plastic quality of the written line, both within the constraints of translation. Kevin Sullivan, who relates this incident, claims that the translation demonstrates "a sense of language that was to mature into genius."[19] As an adult writer Joyce would continue to exploit language's plastic qualities to the fullest, as in a sentence where the subject outrides the syntax as the characters on horses are said to do: "In the saddles of the leaders, leaping leaders, rode outriders" (248). Indeed, this sense of language is the same in the schoolboy assignment as in the mature novel: it is expressive form created through the manipulation of words.

For the Jesuits, Joyce also wrote an essay entitled "The Study of Languages" in which he noted that "both in style and syntax there is always present a carefulness, a carefulness bred of the first implantings of precision."[20] Joyce acknowledged this studied precision and even prided himself on it. To Stanislaus he wrote, "Would you be surprised if I wrote a very good English grammar some day?"[21] As a description of Joyce's attitude to language, Ellman's comment is typical: "At a time others were questioning the liberties he took with English, Joyce was conscious only of its restraints upon him."[22] But being aware of restrictions by no means implies not accepting them; Joyce's "moral nature" may have been egotistical, but it could also be accommodating, and it was precise. To the mob of Russelite mystics Joyce takes a counterstance not only of Aristotelean exactness, the dagger definitions, but also syntactical exactness: "I, who dishevelled ways forsook / To hold the poets' grammar book" ("The Holy Office"). Joyce's was a pride luciferean in rebellion, bred of his knowledge and power to use language and to use it well, which means also to misuse it intelligently. T. S. Eliot claimed that there could be no real blasphemy without there being a deep understanding of the object, and as true as this may be of Joyce's Catholicism, it is no less true of his language in *Ulysses*. It is a language so precise in its use and deviations as to insist on all the rules in the poet's grammar book. Joyce considered *Ulysses* as being written, for all its uniqueness, in a "wideawake language, a cutanddry grammar."[23] To call such sentences as "perfume of embraces all him assailed" or "with hungered flesh obscurely, he mutely craved to adore" (168) cut-and-dry is to insist intelligently and not perversely on the rules they lovingly affront.

Whether Joyce was influenced by any specific linguistic theories during the many years of writing *Ulysses* is largely a matter of conjecture. A general work which was to change thinking about language, Saussure's *Cours de linguistique générale*, was printed in 1916, although Joyce had not read it before finishing *Ulysses*.[24] While in Paris, writing *Work in Progress*, Joyce attended several lectures by a French Jesuit.[25] Mary Colum, who attended with Joyce, describes one of these occasions:

> Abbé Jousse was lecturing in Paris. He was a noted propounder of a theory that Joyce gave adherence to, that language had its origin in gesture—"In the beginning was the rhythmic gesture," Joyce often said.
>
> If the Abbé's lecture did not interest me as much as it interested Joyce, still, it interested me a good deal, and that largely because of its original method of presentation. It took the form of a little play, based on the Gospels. Around the lecturer was a group of girls, who addressed him as "Rabbi Jesus." The words spoken—one of the parables, I think—were, I gathered, in Aramaic, and what was shown was that the word was shaped by the gesture. Joyce was full of the subject.[26]

The date of the lectures comes almost a decade after the publication of *Ulysses*. The specific reference to language as gesture in the "Circe" episode[27] is evidence that Joyce was familiar with the theory before the lectures were given: it is mentioned in *Stephen Hero*. It is perhaps most plausible to consider that, at whatever date, Joyce found the theory congenial because of his own sense of language as conveying meaning in ways other than by denotation. Jousse's theory may have answered to Joyce's practice (and Joyce was never interested in applying other ideas, from Aquinas down, if they did not correspond to his own prior practice). While the Abbé saw lurking behind all spoken language the shadow of original gesture, Joyce saw behind the written word the shadow of expressive form. The schoolboy at Belvedere who was careful to separate the adjective and noun by the end of the line so that they themselves enacted a cliff-hanging showed himself from the outset, long before the Abbé, to be a writer who was aware of language describing and communicating in symbolic formal ways. Early on he recognized that the order of words, or their grouping in the sentence line, conveys meaning, and that their syntactical form can convey a sense more complete than that recognized by Lindley Murray. As Stephen claims in his "theory," language itself renders visible nuance and emotion. Carefully crafted in original patterns, language enacts a meaning and presents what it means in a visual form. With the rules and order of syntax used and misused as its structure, language is an expressive as well as appropriate form.

What can be made of this expressive form, what after all it expresses, and in what way the order of Joyce's unique syntax is appropriate are all questions raised by every sentence in the novel. A sentence like "while his eyes still read blandly he took off his hat quietly inhaling his hairoil" (71) has more lurking behind its syntax than the comedy of ambiguity—whether Bloom blandly read and quietly took off his hat or blandly took off his hat and quietly inhaled —and that effect, not to be captured by statistics, is worthy of consideration.

La Littérature est, et ne peut pas être autre chose qu'une sorte
d'extension et d'application de certaines propriétès du language.

Valéry

Dialectic, the universal language.   *Ulysses*

2 Syntax: Principles and Contexts of Dialectic

Mulling over the seeming illogic of language and its system,
Wittgenstein was moved to ask, offhandedly and hypo-
thetically, "Was tut der, der eine neue Sprache konstruiert
(erfindet), nach welchem Prinzip geht er vor?"[1] (What does
one do when one constructs [invents] a new language?
According to which principle does one proceed?") Wittgenstein thought it important to find the motivating and
guiding principle behind a language, for to recognize that
concept would be to determine the language's lines and
limits, to know what it can and can not do. There is no
evidence that Wittgenstein ever got to the end of this
search, although he did apprehend the limits of logical
language by the time of the "Blue Book." Yet his is a question to be asked of any number of constructed languages,
and especially of Joyce's unique one. It would be hard to
say that Joyce invents a language for *Ulysses* (such a claim
might be valid of *Finnegans Wake*), but it is clear that he
had recast and adapted language in the work to fit his own
expression and particular conceptions: it is the order he
claimed to Budgen was "in every way appropriate." To
recognize the principles which guide the creation of such
idiosyncratic language is to begin to understand the pur-

25

pose and character, the effect and meaning of its particular constructions.

As noted in the previous chapter, the impulse of the Joycean sentence is two-fold, to adhere to the system of syntax and yet to break it. Each sentence is carefully constructed to yield a tension between syntactic order and expressive form, an interplay between relative tight control and creative freedom. Moreover it is clearly Joyce's intent to build this structure of opposites. The Wittgensteinean terminology of principle is appropriate because it suggests the sense that Joyce is consciously making his language in this dual way.

"To no end gathered: vainly then released, forth flowing, wending back: loom of the moon" (49–50). In this example the past tense is set up in contrasted parallel participles, *gathered* and *released;* the opposition of the words is further underscored by the change in time sequence from past to present signaled by the adverb *then.* The present tense is then rendered active in present participles, their grammatically parallel forms offset by the pair of antithetical adverbs *forth* and *back:* "forth flowing, wending back." The rhythm of the passage is repeated in the rhyme and visual echo of the last phrase, "loom of the moon." This example, each phrase an adjectival description of the ebb and flow of waves, is tightly constructed within its loose movement. Its structure belies its free flow just as the mathematical certitude of the sine curve hides the rhythmic poetry of an ocean wave. Similar balance and tension are achieved in the following: "Sour pipe removed he held a shield of hand beside his lips that cooed a moonlight nightcall, clear from anear, a call from afar, replying" (279). The studied order of nouns and prepositions gives regularity to the sentence, while seeming to depict rather than denote the act of shielding the lips. There is also a rhythmic alternation of words, *anear* and *afar,* as well as their sounds, *moonlight nightcall, clear / anear, call* and *afar.* The resultant balance is continued in the beginning and the end of the sentence by a participal phrase as adjective, "sour pipe removed," and absolute present participle, *replying.* Through the careful positioning and refashioning, through his adopted principles, Joyce consciously constructs his language.

A sentence such as the following clearly presents to the reader both the originality of syntactic license and the implied form of proper order, with a result (this time) of comic potential: "At Haddington road corner two sanded women halted themselves, an umbrella and a bag in which eleven cockles rolled to view with wonder the lord mayor and the lady mayoress without his golden chain" (254). Whether the umbrella and bag halted along with the ladies or separately, whether the cockles rolled out of the bag to view the procession with wonder instead of the sanded women, and whether the lady mayoress underwent a change of gender without his chain of mayoralty—all these are questions that the careful disordering of syntax and the connections of proper form pose to the reader. The comic effect is clearly intended and is achieved by the careful and evident control exerted over the syntax of the sentence.

It is in this sense of intent that a large difference emerges between the analysis and appreciation of Joyce's syntax in this study and the methods of transformational grammar. The transformational grammarian looks for the revelation of meaning in hidden structures embedded within (and underneath) the surface of the sentence, structures which are not immediately present to the author's consciously creating mind. The Joycean sentence, as has been seen, has its tensions of syntax clearly on the surface of the sentence, where the author's sense of style is so readily evident. The created tension is intended by the author to be apparent to the reader so that it will be sensed on reading, not on reflecting. Intention and transparency are important to Joyce's principles of language; the balanced structure the artist has so carefully created must be evident.

As a contrast, take this transformational analysis of a "deletion in the tree structure" in one Joyce sentence.

> In the following example, branches labeled AUX [auxiliary verb], N [noun], CONJ [conjunction], REL [relative marker], and PREP [preposition] are deleted: "Boland's breadvan delivering with trays our daily but she prefers yesterday's loaves turnovers crisp crowns hot" (p. 57). The sentence expanded with its deleted parts would read: "Boland's breadvan (AUX) delivering with trays our daily (N) but she prefers yesterday's loaves (CONJ) turnovers (REL) (AUX) crisp (PREP) crowns hot."
>
> Tracing the derivational history of the sentence requires three steps: (1) recover the surface tree, (2) insert the deleted forms by applying stylistic transformations in reverse, (3) associate the proper basic tree, again by reverse transformations.[2]

The steps begin by making the missing word a noun and *daily* its adjective; this yields the noun phrase "our / daily / bread." The author continues: "Upon obtaining the associated basic tree, we find that this segment is a sentence embedded in the larger construction." (That is, "our bread" as noun phrase, with a suppressed *is* and *daily* as a predicate adjective.)

28

This seems to go under rather than go deep. While capturing the implied play on words of "our daily bread," the analysis does away with the tension Joyce so characteristically builds by separating the sentence parts, because it sublimates that tension to a distant, hidden order. Much as in the other examples seen before, the noun qualified by the adjective *daily* has been pushed further ahead (*loaves*), so that the adjective phrase "but she prefers yesterday's" becomes physically as well as grammatically an interjection, qualifying Bloom's use of the plural pronoun *our*. These subtle variations and grammatical tensions of the sentence-line are certainly not resolved by an embedded structure; nor, more importantly, do they follow deep transformational rules. The tensions lie clearly on the surface of the sentence; the manipulated words pull in a variety of ways with the order of syntax. Moreover the principles with which the artist creates (or, as Wittgenstein would say, constructs) his language make that tension apparent. Joyce wants to underscore the limits he transgresses.

The quality here described as the intent to create an obvious tension between syntactic order and disorder suggests a systematic exploitation of language that goes beyond mere originality. When Joyce claimed to Budgen that there was in his language an order in every way appropriate, one that, when created, required an apology to Lindley Murray, he was claiming that his language was appropriate in another way: as a repository of meaning, appropriate in much the same way that the orders of hours, organs, and arts were. The unique syntax of *Ulysses* suggests itself, indeed even thrusts itself forward as a signal of meaning. Its consistency of principle in altering syntax, granted the consistency of Joyce's inconsistency, pervades the entire book and makes a reasonably accessible register of meaning; among the many that apply to the novel it is not the least inconsistent and not the least telling because of its primary function as language.

The expressive form of Joyce's appropriate order is especially articulate. To adopt consciously (and Joyce did nothing without deliberation), to choose a manner of writing which intentionally uses double-edged principles of language ordered and disordered to create meaning, is to take a particular view and make a certain statement about the world articulated through the words. A principled style is not without its implications. Proust, a writer quite different from Joyce, although often compared with him, makes a statement to this point in the last volume of his novel *Le Temps retrouvé:* "le style pour l'écrivain, aussi bien que la couleur pour le peintre, est une question non de technique mais de vision." ("Style for the writer, just as color for the painter, is a question not of technique but of vision.") Language, for the verbal artist, is more than craft. Style is something more than polish and posture. Created along certain principles, it is an articulated vision of the world as the artist sees it, and simultaneously a vision of the world he creates through the style.

Nowhere is Joyce's awareness of the visions of styles better displayed than in the chapter "The Oxen of the Sun," where each historical style (from Latinate English to American slang) operates as more than a pastiche, rather as a particular means of treating the material it conveys. Yet if "Oxen" succeeds in showing that various historical styles each present a different view, the fact was no less true of Joyce's own. Surely he knew it. When Stanislaus tried to interest his brother in the affairs of the world, Joyce retorted, "Don't talk to me about politics. I'm interested only in style."[3] What redeems this statement from an 1890s aestheticism is precisely the awareness Joyce shows that styles involve stances. Style is a form of politics, not in any sense because of being hortatory, but because styles operate on principles of their own, principles which govern the world they treat. A language which orders and disorders, relying on structures while undermining them, is a representation of a political activity of sorts. One thinks of Joyce in terms other than those of politics, but the artist is bound up through his art in a wider realm; as Thomas Mann states through his humanist Settembrini, "So sei auch die Politik mit [Worten] verbunden, oder vielmehr: sie gehe hervor aus dem Bündnis, der Einheit von Humanität und Literatur, denn das schöne Wort erzeuge die schöne Tat."[4] ("Politics is bound with words, or even more: it goes outward from the alliance, from the unity of humanity and literature, since the good word engenders the good deed.") No socialist, no rabble-rouser, rather a scorner of the mob, the artist in Joyce stays aloof, but his is an aloofness not without a stance.

Benjamin Lee Whorf once commented that every language has its own metaphysics,[5] and this is no less true of any particular writer's individual language. Joyce's unique sentences with their characteristic syntax express something about the world of *Ulysses*, make visual certain ways in that world, and give meaning to them. It is not a matter of Joyce's being forced to "break" syntax in order to express the complex modern world, as is widely enough held, but rather of his using a language with a syntax in opposition whose principles are analogous to those in operation in the world. At the level of law and of the artist's creation, the metaphysics of Joyce's syntax becomes the vision of the world that metaphysics dictates.

Thus the language of *Ulysses* has a significance which reverberates beyond the constructions themselves. Hugh Kenner, in his early book *Dublin's Joyce,* claims that "the language of Dublin *is* the subject" of the novel, and he is not far from the mark.[6] Like the principles of light and gravity which stimulate Bloom to much thought and affect his universe, those of language affect the world of the novel. What is recognizable as a principle of syntax can be related by analogy to other parts of the text: the syntax of order and disorder creates an art which is repeatedly characterized by opposition.

The presence of opposition in Joyce's work has now become a fully accepted, even commonplace critical notion. Opposition can be encountered in the very form of the novel: a tension between minute detail and the vastness of epic scope, between the ordained patterns of organs, arts, times, and colors and the occurrences of coincidence and the idiosyncrasies of life. The many themes of *Ulysses* are statable in terms of balanced oppositions; as Ellmann points out in his *Ulysses on the Liffey,* "if one chapter is external, the next is internal, . . . if one episode centres on land, the second will be watery."[7] Many of Joyce's theories, such as they are, concern contradictory notions, for example his attitude toward love as both degrading and uplifting, carnal and spiritual.[8] Joyce admired Bruno, who claimed that the world was divided into opposites. Extending the forms this opposition can take, finding various analogues in the order of chapters or theories of philosophy, is limited only by considerations of time and critical ingenuity. For the purpose here it is sufficient unto the day to note that the syntax of *Ulysses* demonstrates itself to be subject to the same code of opposition that informs all of Joyce's art and may perhaps be, given its progenerative function in that art, the prima facie expression of such opposition.

The facility with which the notion of opposition might be applied to the text can be clearly seen with reference to the characters and their use of language. Language is the essential form for both artist and character, and it is there that the syntax and its opposing principles offer possibilities of a wide range of meaning.

The differences in the personalities of Stephen and Bloom are too well known to need detailing here, but the analogously two-sided nature of Joyce's language provides a new dimension in which to view the complementary figures. They display between them a host of opposites, and in "Ithaca" this is stated succinctly: "What two temperaments did they individually represent? The scientific. The artistic" (683). Both characters are indeed similar to the sentences they speak.[9] Style being the man, their sentences illustrate the respective sides of the two principles that create those sentences and their being as characters as well. There is not a demonstrable statistical frequency to this, as Joyce is ever careful to balance and counterpoise his options, but he does apply one impulse of language more readily to one character than to the other. Stephen's sentences read like the bon mots of the artist (those indeed of Joyce himself): rhetorically balanced, polished, and finished like the marble surfaces of great statues. He is able to mold language, to fashion it into something. He builds ordered forms which move in an increasingly active progression of their own: "a menace, a disarming and a worst-ing" (21), or "a hoard heaped by the roadside: plundered and passing on" (34). The dynamic change from adjective to participial adjective, or from verb to participle, propels the sentences within an artful form. Bloom, on the other hand, always chasing after people and rarely catching them, lagging behind the events of his own life, seems often at the mercy of language's twists and turns; and he is used by language as much as he uses it. His sentences are loose, open to the whims of leaping association and capricious in their syntactical connections; the phrases are not marshalled in order: "The breeders in hobnailed boots, trudging through the litter, slapping a palm on a ripe-meated hindquarter, there's a prime one, unpeeled switches in their hands" (59).

As a further example of opposition there is each character's comments on Shakespeare's language, a reflection of his own use of words and his attitudes toward language. "But then Shakespeare has no rhymes: blank verse. The flow of the language it is. The thoughts" (152). Bloom's colloquial speech ("but then" and the inverted verb and subject) has a halting and abrupt quality; the equation of no rhyme with blank verse reads like the rote repetition of a fact from a textbook. Stephen's, on the other hand, has the completeness of aphorism and copybook entry, neatly parallel and appropriate in diction: "He was himself a lord of language and had made himself a coistrel gentleman" (196).

Yet Stephen and Bloom can also be quite similar in their languages. Just as at several times during the day they begin to approach each other, their paths crossing, so often their sentences come remarkably close together. In this

Joyce unites them, showing their common points, and showing as well the relativity of the principles of syntactic order and disorder. "You will see who" (47), a sentence from Stephen's almost remembered dream, is as conversational in its abruptness as Bloom's comment about privacy, "Hate company when you" (73). At the same time at different bookstalls, their responses to literary works are almost interchangeable.

> Aristotle's *Masterpiece*. Crooked botched print. Plates: infants cuddled in a ball in bloodred wombs like livers of slaughtered cows. (235)

> Binding too good probably, what is this? Eighth and ninth book of Moses. Secret of all secrets. Seal of King David. Thumbed pages: read and read. (242)

Style, construction, even punctuation cannot distinguish between them, and literary tastes may be the only determining factor.

If Bloom and Stephen, in their singularity and in their interchange, seem to represent language's two principles, Molly might represent the extreme of language at its loosest and most flowing. For her, language is less a medium than an indistinguishable part of life, natural and inevitable like sex or death. Her exuberance for love results in an equally exuberant sentence structure: "You sometimes love to wildly when you feel that way so nice all over you can't help yourself" (740). Molly disregards the order of syntax: "lying among the rhododendrons on Howth head in the grey tweed suit" (782); sometimes to a comic effect: "his breakfast in bed with a couple of eggs" (738). She even disdains the restraints of grammar: "that was his studenting" (754). Her world view accordingly encompasses both

35

the whole globe and a little space: "who else from all the ends of Europe and Duke Street" (782).

If Molly's language represents such universality, the narrative voice can often take (among its many tones) an opposite particularity and minute scope. A question and answer sequence at the end of "Ithaca" suggests the rigidity of which that one voice is capable:

> There remained a period of 9 months and 1 day during which in consequence of a preestablished natural comprehension in incomprehension between the con-summated females (listener and issue), complete corporal liberty of action had been circumscribed.
>
> How?
>
> By various reiterated feminine interrogation concerning the masculine destination whither, the place where, the time which, the duration for which, the object with which in the case of temporary absences, projected or effected. (736)

Thus the language of *Ulysses* offers an expression of opposition, one that is most pervasive, given language's primary importance to the text. The principles of syntax as ordered and disordered readily lend themselves to association with (if they do not create) any number of dual terms, and it is some measure of their appropriateness that they do so. Language as both generator and mediator for opposition and duality is most basic to Joyce's conception of art, itself a dialectic of balance and tension.

The *Portrait* closes with Stephen's proud entry in his diary: "Welcome, O Life! I go to encounter for the millionth time the reality of experience and to forge in the smithy of my soul the uncreated conscience of my race."[10] The art he goes forth to create seeks to mediate between

36

the inner world and the outer, in an attempt to offset his individual response with the forms of the larger world outside him. There is in this a confrontation between private and public, ephemeral soul and harsh physical reality, which in the course of the *Portrait* is resolved by the art which finally creates the novel itself. Art attempts, through twisting and shaping, to bring disparate poles together and to present in the figure called the artist a projection of himself in the lines and shadows of his text.

Stephen continues to articulate this notion of duality in art; in his lecturing in the Library in *Ulysses,* he repeats his earlier idea that the soul confronts reality in art, but he amplifies the notion by speaking in Aristotelean terms: "He found in the world without as actual what was in his world within as possible" (213). As he considers the relation of Shakespeare's life to his art, Stephen comes to the full recognition that art combines opposites, that it unifies such disparate elements as the inner world and the outer, soul and reality. Stephen even sees that art unites spirit and matter; he confronts and combines the viewpoints of Æ the mystic and Mulligan the sensualist by arguing his theory.[11]

It is worth noting that Stephen has extended his own terms, freely associating various pairs in his dialectic of art. To the original pair of soul and reality from the *Portrait* he adds that of spirit and matter; these are terms that are hardly equivalent, but ones that can be related. Encouraged by Stephen's own association of terms in his attempt to describe his art, one can extrapolate others, also related if not equivalent, which suggest regulative notions for Joyce's art.[12] Art balances soul or spirit with reality or matter: the spiritual and the physical are offset. It is thus

37

possible to add the pair of intellect (or mind) and body. Consequently, the dialectic of Joyce's art can also embrace mental and physical, intangible and tangible. Ellmann says succinctly of his art: "All may be resolvable into brute body or into mind and mental components," and he adds, "Joyce lived between the antipodes and above them."[13]

The applicability of syntax's appropriate order extends even to these various terms of dialectic. It is Joyce's language, after all, which enables his art to combine opposites; dialectic is "the universal language" for art as well as for argument. Hence the dual principles of that language lend themselves readily to association with the various dialectical pairs. Order in syntax would appear to answer to order in the reality of experience and the material world of systems and bodies; the free constructions, open and unlimited, suggest the ineffability and uniqueness of soul or mind. That this is indeed the case, subsequent chapters will demonstrate: syntax's expressive form can represent each term in the dialectic. Yet as the very principles themselves were demonstrated to be relative, depending on the context, so too are the associations which can be made between those principles and the various dialectic terms. The order and disorder of syntax can enact either the physical or mental in the dialectic; which term applies depends on the context in which it figures at any given point.

The dialectic discussed with reference to Stephen's theories in the several paragraphs above is one concerned with the artistic endeavor: the artist, making his art, seeks to yoke spirit and matter, soul and reality. He combines the particular responses of his spirit with the matter of the world around him; he seeks to recreate that reality in his art by shaping it in the smithy of his soul—or "in the womb of the imagination," as Stephen says, conflating the opposite powers of intellect and body—to create his art and his own self within that art. Yet the same dialectic holds true within the created world of the novel, and the characters are engaged in an analogous endeavor.

Each character (like the character Stephen *within* the *Portrait*) also goes forth to experience life in the course of a novel; and in confronting it he seeks to transform it in the crucible of his soul. (And to what other end does the technique of interior monologue work but to show within each character just this interaction of outer reality and inner thought?) Bloom and Stephen, as characters in *Ulysses*, are both artists in this analogous sense, that they seek to combine their individual responses to the world outside them, to unify soul and reality, spirit and matter, in the human endeavor which is their daily (if fictional) lives.

It is language which is essential to both these dialectical endeavors. The characters clearly owe their whole existence, mind and body both, to language; they are postulated by it, and their lives are invested and circumscribed by the very medium that creates them. The artist is similarly constituted: it is only through language that he can resolve the dialectic of soul and reality, and it is only through language that he can project his being, as language gives substance to his figure and voice to his ideas. The entity called artist, the one who can be seen intentionally manipulating the syntax of sentences, is recognized by the changes he rings on the text: he projects himself and reveals himself through language.

Language's syntax is the salient form in these dialectics

of essence and identity. It gives expression to the dialectic for both character and artist and it is the means by which one can recognize their presence in the text. Each principle of syntax enacts one part of the dialectic for the artist, engaged in his endeavor to combine mind and body, spirit and matter, and another for the characters, in their encounter with the reality created by the artist in the text (and in opposition to what the syntax enacts with reference to the artist).

The appropriate order of expressive form in syntax thus creates a context in which both artist and character are involved, as they are involved in a similar dialectical endeavor. Yet that context is marked not only by the opposition of the relative positions of artist and character, but also by the differing powers of each. As will become increasingly evident in the subsequent analyses, the artist retains control not only of his text but also of his language and its created dialectic. He is able to create; his characters are only part of the creation. He has the potential to act; they are restrained by their situation in language. He is free to make both order and disorder; they are bound by that order and disorder.

Ultimately, the principles of Joyce's syntax enrich the dialectic at the core of his art by adding further tension and opposition. The principles of syntax, in their various manifestations of order and license, counterbalance valent forces at different levels: they offset not only inner world and outer, soul and reality, mind and body, but also artist and character, creator and text; and the syntax is the register of recognizing and of assigning meaning to these contexts.

In the passage following, the expressive richness in

40

acknowledging a dialectic context made both possible and manifest by the appropriate order of syntax is readily apparent. The thoughts of Bloom's monologue alternate in increasing rapidity with the statements of the narrative voice, one projection of the artist-figure. The character is clearly recognized by references in the first person, the artist's voice by the third:

> Look for something I.
> His hasty hand went quick into a pocket, took out, read unfolded *Agendath Netaim*. Where did I?
> Busy looking for.
> He thrust back quickly Agendath.
> Afternoon she said.
> I am looking for that. Yes, that. Try all pockets. Handker. *Freeman*. Where did I? Ah, yes. Trousers. Purse. Potato. Where did I?
> Hurry. Walk quietly. Moment more. My heart.
> His hand looking for the where did I put found in his hip pocket soap lotion have to call tepid paper stuck. Ah, soap there! Yes. Gate.
> Safe! (183)

Yet, as the passage moves to its final pronouncement of Bloom's relief, the space of syntax between the two becomes increasingly compressed to the point finally of an alternation of phrases: "looking for the / where did I put / found . . . hip pocket soap / lotion I have to call." The narrative voice's sentence would probably be "His hand looking for the soap found (it) in his hip pocket with tepid paper stuck (on)"; Bloom's "Where did I put (the soap); lotion I have to call for. Ah Soap! There in my hip pocket" (with his characteristic inversion of predicate and verb). The compression of both sentences, and the characteristic loosening of word order, accommodates and combines both creator and character in a texture filled with indications of meaning on various levels—thematic as well as syntactic. In the opposition of *put / found* or in the pair by association *soap / lotion* one finds the expressive form of syntax, where the dialectic between character and artist is made apparent.

To consider the play of the principles of syntax, then, and to consider what those principles represent in the contexts of the artist figure and character, is to suggest the meaning of *Ulysses* in terms of the appropriate order of its expressive form. The validity of such a contention is not, of course, readily apparent. There are various indices of meaning for the novel—so large a novel admits of any number of ways of assessing its significance. Yet such a contention takes it justification from several factors. Foremost is the primacy and consistency of syntax in all parts of the novel; there is not one character, not one theme, not one parallel that is not created by a language clearly unique in its own order. What has heretofore been demonstrated is also pertinent: Joyce's clear and careful manipulation of language into an expressive form, his creation of that symbolic form according to certain principles, and his sense of a verbal art mediating in a variety of dialectics both for his characters and for himself as artist-figure.

The form of Joyce's sentences and their principles suggest a sense of the life and world of *Ulysses*. Joyce could subscribe to such an idea. More than a vehicle for the demonstration of the views of styles, the symbolism of the foetus in the "Oxen of the Sun" contains an important parallel that animates and motivates that chapter: Joyce's conviction that life and language are analogous and parallel systems and processes, that they share common movements and structures. Art imitates life not by copying it faintly, but more importantly by enacting life through its expressive form. The dialectic within art embraces both life and language, reality and its expression. There can be (and ought to be) a transfer of the structures of language to the novel, a concordance of the laws that govern language with those that rule over the artist and the created universe of his work.

This is a hypothesis that seems hyperbolic, but—understatement hardly being the Joycean method—such a hypothesis can carry far into an understanding of the novel. Vico, whose ideas were very important to Joyce in the creating of his art, claimed that all history was recoverable through etymology.[14] This study would like to turn the tables on Joyce, and view the meaning of his novel as recoverable through its syntax. To consider the whole of *Ulysses* in this way, even if by means of occasionally tenuous analogy, is to weigh it in terms of its strength, the power of its verbal creation. Then what is often considered a literary masterpiece devoid of human perspective precisely because of its verbal technique comes to reveal meaning when viewed by means of, and in terms of, its language. Joyce's order is appropriate in many ways.

In addition (and this is a large advantage), a broad perspective on *Ulysses* reached in terms of its particular words, its every line, restores some degree of integrity and wholeness to the novel. *Ulysses*, perhaps more than any other work of art and certainly more than any other novel, has spawned generations of guides which attempt, and with some success, to trace the meaning of the novel by explaining various allusions within the text to other works. While performing a noteworthy function in assessing the

43

book's meaning, such guides have the inevitable tendency of overstressing the novel's own outward-directed dimension, as the various allusions cause the reader to move vertically out and away from the story line to other texts to find meaning. Yet there is meaning to be found within the language itself that moves linearly into becoming the novel. The sense of language engaged in two dimensions is original with Saussure,[15] but Joyce anticipates this brilliant concept of syntagm and paradigm through no less a formidable critic and astute user of language than the canvasser Leopold Bloom: "The infinite possibilities hitherto unexploited of the modern art of advertisement if condensed in triliteral monoideal symbols, vertically of maximum visibility (divined), horizontally of maximum legibility (deciphered) and of magnetising efficacy to arrest involuntary attention, to interest, to convince, to decide" (683).

It is now fitting to turn to the deciphering of the syntactic line, and to the analysis of the meaning of the specific structures Joyce creates, which themselves, like the art of potent advertising in their magnetizing efficacy, provoke attention, convince, and decide by means of their expressive, appropriate order.

Seat of the affections. Broken heart. A pump after all, pumping thousands of gallons of blood every day.

Gasballs spinning about, crossing each other, passing. Same old dingdong always. *Ulysses*

3 Order as Patterns

"The disk shot down the groove, wobbled a while, ceased and ogled them: six" (229). Tom Rochford's machine for informing the dancing public of the "Turn Now On" is not of any great importance in *Ulysses*. Yet it becomes quite apposite when one considers the mechanical, patterned elements which abound in the novel. The machine appears in one of the most arbitrarily ordered chapters, the central "Wandering Rocks," where the complexity of the novel as a whole is so clearly reflected. The disk that stares so rudely at Lenehan, Flynn and M'Coy—themselves a rude group—shares with the novel the quality of machinery's systemic and orderly effrontery.

The patterns of *Ulysses* are anything but hidden. The process of composition of the work, probably because of its inordinate complexity, moved along rigid lines, as A. Walton Litz has made abundantly clear in his detailed examination of the making of the novel. Joyce's many note sheets, from those in the British Museum to those taken on his cuff, assured, in Litz's words, "that patterns and relations already visualized by Joyce reached their fore-ordained positions in the text." He continues: "The mechanical nature of this process emphasizes the mechanical nature of those ordering principles which give *Ulysses* its superficial unity."[1] Everything has its place and, in the encyclopaedic embrace of the novel, there is a place for everything. The schemes of organs and arts are less important in themselves than as means of organization. Budgen recounts Joyce's describing his mode of composition: "In 'Lestrygonians' the stomach dominates. . . . Walking towards his lunch . . . Bloom thinks of his wife, and says to himself, 'Molly's legs are out of plumb.' At another time of day he might have expressed the same thought without any underthought of food."[2] Joyce was not usually noted for such modesty; in another chapter it would be the writer who would have the character express himself differently. The overall plan, which makes its appearance in the text in often sporadic ways, probably functions as scaffolding and direction; the Homeric parallels, for example, are most useful as signs for, rather than keys to, interpretation. Ezra Pound early and astutely, if somewhat abruptly, realized this: "The parallels with the *Odyssey* are mere mechanics, any blockhead can go back and trace them."[3]

The novel also unveils before the reader a mechanics of structure. Three chapters in an opening section, three in a closing, twelve in the main, the tenth central chapter a miniature replication of the others—these patterns all combine to a superficial balance of mere numbers. Yet the different form that each chapter takes, the striving for a pluralism, militates against a unified interpretation along those lines. The essential aim of the patterned formalism of the chapters may well be an arbitrary diversity. Between the typographical mechanics of the headlines of "Aeolus" and the catechism of "Ithaca" lies a whole world of other, perhaps exclusive, forms: musical, as in "Sirens"; dramatic, as in "Circe"; or dialectic, as in "Scylla." The order and relation of the forms may, like the compositional schemes, be more arbitrary than significant.

All of the above is by now an indispensable part of Joyce criticism, but something has gone unrecognized. In Joyce's statement to Budgen on the order in every way appropriate of the words on the page, the emphasis is as much on order as on propriety. What exists as orders and plans at the levels of composition and structure in the novel is reflected basically in the patterns stressed by Joyce's language. Syntactic order is itself pattern and system, and by emphasizing and exploiting that order the material of the novel can be organized and presented in a particularly emphatic way. Syntax's accountability, its marshalling of parts into a whole, infuses the novel with a sense of control. That control is necessary for the artist: with it, he gives his sentences meaning, proportion, and effect; using it, he creates a functional, even vital, order in the text for the characters. Yet he can also stress that control to the point that it becomes as arbitrary in its application for the characters as the larger systems described above do for the reader. The order of language is for Joyce an order both functionally useful and potentially capricious.

What Joyce recognized in his artistic practice was probably reinforced by his teaching of English during the early composition of the book. Benjamin Lee Whorf notes that "the attempt to teach one's language to a foreigner results in some awareness of OVERT formal patterns."[4] A glance at a Berlitz textbook of the period of Joyce's teaching discovers sentences which, while stressing the forms of English, look very much like the art of *Ulysses:* "Before whom? Before me, you, him, her. Who? I am you are he is

47

she is—sitting, standing."[5] The textbooks of Berlitz and of Lindley Murray stand behind many of the novel's constuctions. It is through such highly apparent use of the order of syntax and the structures of language that Joyce works a most suggestive patterning into the life of the novel.

At the basic verbal level many of the "word games" in the text are based on the patterns of language. Language itself is the subject of this declension: "in words, of words, for words" (200). Several possible parts of a word—as subject, object or verb—are in this sentence: "Drinkers, drinking, laughed spluttering, their drink against their breath" (167). Similarly, the same verb is given new meaning by repeated use: "For all things dying, want to, dying to, die" (286). Making nouns from adjectives and adverbs is the exercise of this "Brownean" style: "Region of remoteness the whatness of our whoness hath fetched his whenceness" (394). There are tricks played with compound words: "She poured in a teacup tea, then back in the teapot tea" (258).

The novel is replete with many such tricks on the patterns of word parts. The librarian Lyster is described answering a request: "O! Father Dineen! Directly. Swiftly rectly creaking rectly rectly he was rectly gone" (211). Various words suggest themselves as the adverbs; as well as the obvious *directly*, there is *correctly*, and even *rectly* as a rector. A common etymological source is played upon here: "Which example did he adduce to induce Stephen to deduce" (684). Often a prefix is strung out in a pattern of different words: "multicoloured multiform multitudinous garments" (729), or "mulberrycoloured, multicoloured, multitudinous vomit" (217), where the first term has only a visual, not an etymological similarity. Visual repetition, as well as rhythmic and morphemic patterning, characterize these examples: "lovesoft oftloved" (274); "lionel loneliness" (275); "manless moonless womoonless marsh" (283); "from afar, from farther out" (46).

At the end of "Circe" Bloom turns to Corny Kelleher for help with the unconscious Stephen. The refrain of "tooraloom" sung by Kelleher, which appears often in the novel, plays throughout the passage in replication of grammatical forms of a verb: "Kelleher reassures [Bloom]. . . . The car jingles tooraloom round the corner of the tooraloom lane. Corny Kelleher again reassuralooms with his hand. Bloom with his hand assuralooms Corny Kelleher that he is reassuraloomtay" (608). Stephen walks along the beach in "Proteus" treading on the sea wrack: "crush, crack, crick, crick" (37); it is a walk in progress which, in its onomatopoeia, echoes the progression from past to present of English verbs. Bloom, inspired by the music of the "Sirens," thinks erotically: "Tipping her tepping her tapping her topping her" (274).

This last example can also serve by way of introducing a more substantive way in which the patterns of language are used in the novel. The example brings out clearly the mimetic and representational ability, the expressive form of Joyce's language: it has a surface pattern of the order of vowels, but that patterning lends itself to the enactment of a process as active and rhythmic as the sexual one to which the phrases refer. The expressive form of Joyce's syntax is highly plastic, and through the principles of its order it enables Joyce to portray vividly the life within the novel; with it he can express the primacy of human experience—or, to use Stephen's terms, he can create the "reality of experience." The constructions of a tightened order, precisely because of their own patterns, can imitate what is most mechanical and patterned in life; through the expressive form of ordered structures certain physical activities and processes can be enacted.[6] It is undeniable that Joyce sought out patterns in his art; patterns were for him methods of organizing and presenting material. More importantly, he sought both the patterns of syntax and those of language itself because they enable him not only to present but also to enact the material world of his novel in a vivid and realistic way.

By its particular patterning the language easily recreates that which is itself most patterned. Hair is described mimetically as "wavyavyeavyheavyeavyevyevy" (277). Stephen thinks of distance, and the language enacts it: "wayaway-awayawayawayaway" (48). The object in this following sentence seems grammatically to imitate the birds it represents in soaring away from its subject and verb: "Looking down he saw flapping strongly, wheeling between the gaunt quay walls, gulls" (152). Stephen sees two cockle pickers on the beach at a great distance from him, and the syntax pushes the subjects equally far away: "From farther away, walking shoreward across from the crested tide, figures, two" (45). Here indeed the form follows the content: "An Inchicore tram unloaded straggling highland soldiers of a band" (228); the jumbled order of words replicates the disorderly disembarking of the instrument-loaded band players who later "blare and drumthump" at the royal procession. Equally imitative because of its syntax is this description of the outriders in the same carriage procession who seem to sit unevenly in their grammatical saddles: "Outriders leaping, leaping in their, in their saddles" (241).

This example from "Aeolus" employs a rhetorical device,

as is fitting for the chapter, yet the content it describes lifts the artful construction from mere rhetorical display: "Grossbooted draymen rolled barrels dullthudding out of Prince's stores and bumped them up the brewery float. On the brewery float bumped dullthudding barrels rolled by grossbooted draymen out of Prince's stores" (116). The physical action of barrels being rolled up and down a ramp is accurately mimed by the language. The circular movement of outgoing and incoming trams is also reproduced by syntax: "Right and left parallel clanging ringing a doubledecker and a singledeck moved from their railheads, swerved to the down line, glided parallel" (116). In much the same manner of construction as well as in the same quality of machinery, the parallel order of the railroad and the pattern of its tracks are copied in this: "Retreating, at the terminus of the Great Northern Railway, Amiens street, with constant uniform acceleration, along parallel lines meeting at infinity, if produced: along parallel lines, reproduced from infinity, with constant uniform retardation, at the terminus of the Great Northern Railway, Amiens street returning" (730).

Nature itself abounds in patterns analogous to and readily reproduced by language. Stephen, in his reflective walk on the beach, comments artfully on the process of alternation in life: "God becomes man becomes fish becomes barnacle goose becomes featherbed mountain" (50). The repetition of verb and the change of subject reinforce the sense of the chain of being, which, when it descends away from God, descends into pure matter; the sentence reproduces the grand design of life. One critic uses this sentence as an example of "branching" in Joyce's writings, but says no more.[7] What he fails to consider is that the term from deep-structure linguistics is inadequate to described why such a construction exists in language or in Joyce's language. "Branching" would seem to arise from the sense of interdependent connection, either between the same subjects with different verbs, or (as here) similar verbs with changing subjects. Joyce uses this construction precisely because it imitates and replicates a sense of nature, and does so in concrete syntactical terms, through carefully stressed patterns. The alternation of ringing bells is reproduced by similar means, where the repeated order of prepositions creates the rhythmical echo: "The sound of the peal of the hour of the night by the chime of the bells of the church of Saint George" (704).

Joyce employs the control and order of his language to present and to stress a very important and specific dimension of the natural world in his novel: the purely, wholly physical existence of his characters, their part in the dialectic of his art. *Ulysses* is a book that hardly flinches from a commitment to the reality of experience in the most literal sense of the word, the frank treatment of the physical aspects of life. In the novel the characters perform a full range of natural physical acts: eating, evacuating, masturbating. The physical basis of all life which lies behind every higher human activity is brought forward into the open in the novel. Joyce reveled in the physical, in the corporeal, perhaps as a contrast to Catholic dogma that would suppress the body; as an artist he welcomed life and the reality in which it consisted. A celebration of the variety and freedom of the body might thus be expected, but Joyce has a different emphasis. Rather than celebrate the possibilities of the body in its manifold variety, he celebrates physical life in terms of its systemic regularity, its orderly processes. In his language, the expressive form of syntax in its patterned order clearly and graphically presents the physicality of the patterned aspects of natural human life. Language lets Joyce recreate life for his characters with due regard for its orderly reality.

The most basic functions of the human body are valued and raised to the level of art by a language which most lovingly reenacts them. Bloom's eating is an example of such a physical activity rendered by patterns in language. "Wine soaked and softened rolled pith of bread mustard a moment mawkish cheese" (174). This renders Bloom's synaesthetic response, the word *mawkish* adding a real taste to the description. The ragout of phrases replicates Bloom's chewing, the automatic mixing and mincing of food by the jaws; a word like *wine* is both a separate entity as noun and as adjective a quality describing the bread, "wine soaked," in a culinary and grammatical concoction. Similarly, phonemic patterns stress the act of chewing in another example from the same chapter: "I munched hum un thu unchster Bunk un Munchday" (170).

Bloom has an immediate physical response to drinking wine: "dribbling a quiet message from his bladder came to go to do not to do there to do" (176). The rhythmic alternation and contradiction of the verbs, created by patterns of language and reinforced through a play on sound, seem to replicate the contractions and relaxations of the bladder itself. Stuart Gilbert notes that "the technic of the episode ('Lestrygonians') is based on a process of nutrition: *peristalsis*, 'the automatic muscular movement consisting of wavelike contractions.'"[8] True to this underlying concept of the presentation of the physical, Joyce uses a similar pattern of language in rhythmic alternation to describe

Bloom in the outhouse, although the "technic" of the chapter "Calypso" calls for something different ("narrative, mature"): "Quietly he read, restraining himself, the first column and, yielding but resisting, began the second. Midway, his last resistance yielding, he allowed" (69). Stephen's urinating (or thought of urinating) is rendered both by alliteration and by changing participles and echoes the waves around him on the Strand: "In cups of rocks it slops: flop, slop, slap. . . . It flows purling, widely flowing, floating foampool, flower unfurling" (49).

Bloom's total physical moment, his orgasm during the fireworks, is replicated by a language which, if arch and coy in its sly reference to the fireworks, is candid and unequivocating in its imitation of the physical quality of the event: "And then a rocket sprang and bang shot blind and O! then the Roman candle burst and it was like a sigh of O! and everyone cried O! O! in raptures and it gushed out of it a stream of rain gold hair threads and they shed and ah! they were all greeny dewy stars falling with golden, O so lively! O so soft, sweet, soft!" (366–67). This is a climax in many senses of the word; it is an explosion of sounds: "a sigh of O! and everyone cried O! . . . O so soft, sweet, soft!" More importantly, it is an emphatic tension of syntax: "and then a rocket sprang and . . . shot blind and." This tension is prepared for in a similar manner throughout the sentences preceding the ones cited. Such a tightened order gives way at the end to a flow of phrases: "a stream of rain gold hair threads and they shed and ah! they were all greeny dewy stars."

Sex is of course crucial to *Ulysses*. A book concerned with physical life, pledged to the reality of experience, cannot but be interested in sexuality. The novel is centered on an act of adultery and it also contains a birth, illicit if distant affairs with young girls, and contact (conversational if not physical) with prostitutes. In the physical world which Joyce seeks to portray through his expressive language, sex is the fundamental expression, and thus it figures prominently in the patterns of language which correspond to the physical.

Bloom's worshipful kiss of Molly's rump and its effects on him in the closing of the "Ithaca" chapter are carefully reproduced by the order of syntax to create an exact (if clinical) expression of arousal:

> The visible signs of antesatisfaction?
> An approximate erection: a solicitous adversion: a gradual elevation: a tentative revelation; a silent contemplation.
>
> Then?
> He kissed the plump mellow yellow smellow melons of her rump, on each plump melonous hemisphere, in their mellow yellow furrow, with obscure prolonged provocative melon-smellonous osculation.
>
> The visible signs of postsatisfaction?
> A silent contemplation: a tentative velation: a gradual abasement: a solicitous aversion: a proximate erection. (734–35)

In the overall perspective of "Ithaca," Bloom's resigned acceptance of the fact of adultery is rendered in a very striking manner: "the natural grammatical transition by inversion involving no alteration of sense of an aorist preterite proposition (parsed as masculine subject, monosyllabic onomatopœic transitive verb with direct feminine object) from the active voice into its correlative aorist preterite proposition (parsed as feminine subject, auxilliary verb and quasimonosyllabic onomatopœic past participle with complimentary masculine agent) in the passive voice" (734). In this example lies a justification for Joyce's analogy connecting language and life; as sex is the generator of life, Joyce indicates that language is a generator as well. Both are structured along analogous patterns and are consequently reflective of each other's processes. As in the natural grammatical inversion of voice, there can be and is an interchangeability of the actors in the process, with a natural physical balance between activity and passivity. Connections are expressed reciprocally, actors require something on which to act, objects receive the attention of actors, and all these are part of a system of nature and life which the patterns of language here so clearly reflect. There is a constant give and take in all relationships, sex being merely the most physical and evident. Bloom makes this point when he tenderly remembers courting Molly on Howth (in a long lyrical passage): "She kissed me. I was kissed" (176); and when he thinks of love as "lips kissed, kissing kissed" (67). The pattern of language from active verb to passive participle adumbrates the relationship, regardless of the particular style of the chapter; through the expressive form of an ordered language the analogous patterns of human interaction are made evident. In a reverie of music and memory, Bloom recognizes the alternation of relationships through the corresponding rhythmic impulse of language, which alternates opposite verbs, and nouns with verbs: "Ha, give! Take! Throb, a throb" (274). Life as a series of connections, of alternations, of balances is figured in a mimetic language ordered in patterns: for every matrimonial violator there must be, as "Ithaca" intones, a "matrimonial violated."

56

Men are interrelated. There is an undeniable connection between Bloom and Boylan besides the agency of Molly. Boylan is hailed by Lenehan as "the conquering hero"; the narrator calls Bloom "the unconquered hero" (264). The language, in its systemic change of a negative prefix, also brings them together, showing how clearly they are aligned, while giving Bloom the palm. Playing with the patterns of language, specifically here the addition of a negative prefix, Joyce expresses all the differences between the two men: while one conquers the other remains unconquerable. Boylan and Bloom are caught together in certain circumstances, related by any number of facts and acts. Not only do they share the same woman, they also have the same tailor. The random connections of life within the novel are reinforced and emphasized by Joyce in the patterns of language; men are no less connected by their grammar. The realization Bloom comes to about adultery in "Ithaca" is bred by the recognition of the interdependence and endless sequence of people caught up together in common experience, and is expressed in language similarly related and parallel: "Each imagining himself to be first, last, only and alone, whereas he is neither first nor last nor only nor alone in a series originating in and repeated to infinity" (731).

It is of course the city of Dublin, the locus which gives the book its genius, which draws all the people together; Dublin the small town where everyone knows everyone else, the small town which looked even smaller from the exile's perspective of a continent away. It is a city where Bloom continually meets his rival Boylan, or pale copies of himself such as M'Coy; where Stephen meets avatars of his father like Gumley, or of himself, his sister Dilly. Like

57

Socrates, each person leaves his doorstep to go out to the city, only to return through others to himself. Man, the *vir urbanus*, exists in many connections: father, friend, foe; in this context one remembers that Joyce chose Odysseus because he was the "complete" man.[9] The many people of Dublin are bound together in patterns of language, society, family. If the artist sees these as nets to trap him personally, through a language artfully manipulated and emphasized he can also turn them into the threads and ties that connect the lives of his characters.

In so doing, he creates structures with language that are analogous to those in the society the novel portrays, yet another function of the expressive form of Joyce's language, a wider representation of the actual life of the novel. The interrelations and connections of the grammatical parts within a sentence are an embodiment and a symbolization of the interdependent relations of the individuals in the world described in that language, what Bloom calls the "domain of interindividual relations" (667).

Pronouns signifying persons are important for this effect. Patently a symbol and a marker, a pronoun emphasizes structure and pattern. A pronoun acts as subject, is acted upon as direct object, and is furthermore an object related through various prepositions. Placement and integration of pronouns into the patterns of language's expressive form are symbolic representations of the individuals they represent and the integration of those individuals into the world of the novel.

The pronouns in the following examples stress the individuals, insist, as it were, on their presence in interaction. Delivering tea to the Ormond Bar, the boots from the hotel, an insignificant figure, resents the snubbing by the two

haughty barmaids. "The boots to them, them in the bar,
them barmaids came. For them unheeding him he banged
on the counter his tray of clattering china" (258). The
women, as sirens, are the center of attention; the boots
comes to them, running an errand for them. Yet the boots
asserts his presence by forcibly making noise to draw attention; he, the only subject, acts with his means (the tray)
in some sign of his existence. In Stephen's consideration
of Aristotle on the existence of bodies, pronouns emphasize
an objectification, even a reification: "He was aware of
them bodies before of them coloured" (37). In the melting
pot of the unconscious in "Circe," the difficulties of identity and sex role are typified in this comment by Circe's
wand, the fan: "Was then she him you us since knew? Am
all them and the same now we?" (528). Every pronoun is
represented, as either subject (*I* indicated by the verb) or
object. If the antecedents of these pronouns are not immediately clear, Bloom can find them among his many ac-
quaintances.

Prepositions have a very important function in this
scheme, for they relate the pronoun to the surroundings,
representing the person's connections to things around
him. The combination of pronoun and preposition is used
symbolically to fix the person into place, into the larger
pattern of life. The prepositions are often stressed by being
separated into phrases. Here is a not uncommon passage
relating to Bloom spoken by the night watch in "Circe":
"Bloom. Of Bloom. For Bloom. Bloom" (453). The watch
marches to this beat, and it is the rhythm of Bloom's life.
Indeed, Bloom's life figured in language seems in some
way a grammatical case in the accusative; in this example
he exists in various cases of the singular.[10] Hunted or

haunted by others, Bloom is always involved with life, always caught up with it in any number of possible connections. Bloom goes to Kiernan's to meet with Cunningham and discuss benefits for the widow of Dignam, and there he is cursed by the Citizen; he goes to the hospital to see Mina Purefoy and is caught up with the medicos. Going in one context, he becomes involved in another. One expects the rest of the watch's march to run, "To Bloom, from Bloom," but hardly "With Bloom." Yet the isolation and ostracism of Bloom which readers feel so acutely is in some measure lessened by the fact that Bloom does exist in these various grammatical connections. While he may be shunned by many and never referred to by his first name, the language, stressing its patterns, works for his integration into the life of the novel. Bloom speaks with Murray, one of the editors at the paper, and senses a fleeting moment of companionship with him through the linking of language.

> —Of course, if he wants a par, Red Murray said
> earnestly, a pen behind his ear, we can do him one.
> —Right, Mr. Bloom said with a nod. I'll rub that in.
> We. (117)

This integration is achieved because the sum of all men in their connections is a community, an entity perhaps unstable, certainly harder to define than a nation. The community is represented by and emphasized through the language which is shared by and embraces everyone; through the patterns of language Joyce unites his diverse characters.

Four o'clock at the Ormond Bar is Bloom's evil hour, the time of the meeting of Blazes and Molly, and Bloom is further put upon by an accidental meeting with Goulding, which causes him to be at the same place as his rival. Despite the loneliness of Bloom in this chapter—the soon to be cuckolded "last sardine Bloom alone"—there is a sense of union achieved through the language. Goulding's invitation to Bloom is one of the few acts of kindness paid to him in the course of the long day, and it ought to be remembered that Goulding is himself a pariah to his brother-in-law, the popular Simon Dedalus. (Simon insulted his wife's brother in front of Bloom on the ride to the cemetery.) Goulding invites Bloom to go for a meal; heretofore Bloom had eaten only alone, at home or at Byrne's. (The sharing of a meal is an ancient ritual of community; the *Odyssey* contains many ceremonial suppers.)[11] "Bite by bite of pie he ate Bloom ate they ate. Bloom and Goulding, married in silence, ate" (269). Sharing the meal brings the men together in a common activity. The two separate entities, *he* (Goulding) and Bloom unite into a couple, *they*. The participle *married* only reinforces what the language has already done. If it is a silent marriage, one perhaps for the convenience of two lonely men, it still brings them together in a small moment of union, as short as the span of a meal, but a union all the same.

While eating, both Bloom and Goulding are cut off from the other members of Dublin's community, being isolated in the dining room away from the bar. What brings all of the people in Dublin together, people on all levels, is their common interest in music and their common experience of song. Everyone in Dublin loves song, from Kelleher's refrain of "tooraloom" to Boylan's "Yorkshire Rose." Song is, of course, language placed in a highly formal pattern. The art of this particular chapter is music, and the form a *fuga per canonem*, a fugue according to the laws. This is art very closely bound to rules and patterns.

When Simon Dedalus is finally persuaded by his cronies to sing, Goulding asks the waiter to open the door so that he and Bloom may hear. In the wonderful manner of coincidence, Simon sings an aria from "Martha" just as Bloom is to write to his secret correspondent. The song weaves through Bloom's thoughts, and presumably those of others. The seductive, emotive charms combine each private man into a group: "touching their still ears with words, still hearts of their each his remembered lives" (273–74). The music moves with prepositions "everywhere all soaring all around about the all, the endlessnessnessness" (276), to its consummation. There it unites the singer with his listener, and the two even with the character in the song: "Siopold," Simon, Lionel, Leopold. The song joins two fathers, one who is left without a son, the other whose son left him. Indeed, it unites listeners everywhere into one: the pronoun *all* is communal as well as democratic. "Come. All clapped. She ought to. Come. To me, to him, to her, you too, me, us" (276). Song, its muse, the figure of Martha, even the sirens who lurk behind the reef of this chapter, come to all of the Dubliners, each separate one, male and female, each individual and highly idiosyncratic "me," and unite them into a community of art and emotion. Music unites all opposites: "We are their harps. I. He. Old. Young" (271). In this context the language performs its task with the same suggestively emotional patterning as music itself.

Misery and family are strong ties which unite the unfortunate in Dublin. Stephen, guilty of ignoring and disdaining his family, admits his connection to it through a terse language.

> —Here, Stephen said. It's all right. Mind Maggy doesn't pawn it on you. I suppose all my books are gone.
> —Some, Dilly said. We had to.
> She is drowning. Agenbite. Save her. Agenbite. All against us. She will drown me with her, eyes and hair. Lank coils of seaweed hair around me, my heart, my soul. Salt green death.
> We.
> Agenbite of inwit. Inwit's agenbite.
> Misery! Misery! (243)

He participates in the slow drowning of his family. He tries to retain a piece of himself, "my books," but the sinking of his sister weights him down and captures him: "She will drown me; . . . hair around me." He cannot stay above the family nor escape by twisting words: "Agenbite of inwit. Inwit's agenbite." He is tied to it by the bonds of language, "We."

Another important common ground for the various and varied Dubliners, along with food and song, is conversation. From the ornate oratory in "Aeolus" to the vitriol in "Cyclops," discussion and debate unite. Stephen fights his way with proud insistence through his argument about Shakespeare, while his audience follows him, if diffidently. Stephen describes them: "They list. Three. They. I you he they" (208). Whatever differences they have among themselves or toward Stephen's theory—and there is an enormous gap in the listeners between, say, Eglinton and Mulligan—they are brought together, enthralled in discussion. Stephen even couples himself in colloquy with his image of Aristotle: "A garland of grey hair on his comminated head see him me clambering down to the footpace" (40).

Perhaps the most important example of the union of men symbolized and brought about through language can be found in "Ithaca." Standing together in mute adoration of the shining star of Molly's lamp, Bloom and Stephen turn to each other: "Both then were silent? Silent, each contemplating the other in both mirrors of the reciprocal flesh of theirhisnothis fellowfaces" (702). The fragile balance of the two separate men finally brought together by the contrary events of the long day is delicately poised in the subject-object pair *each* and *other*. Flesh, the human contact, is indeed here made of words. The two are joined in the reflected combination ("both mirrors") of their "fellowfaces," that is to say their corresponding, counterpart faces, and also their friendship ("fellow") faces. The language sums it up best in the conglomerated *theirhisnothis*, which makes two *(their)* out of one *(his)* by undoing the individual *(not his)*. It is the fine integration of an individual with his counterpart, maintaining the sense of his uniqueness; and it can perhaps only be made in a language which deals in patterns and stresses them. There is the sense as well that the word might be made up of these parts: "their / his / no / this"; it demonstratively points to something which is each, and both, and something more. Language has done here what the society of Dublin could hardly achieve; it has united Stephen and Bloom.

These are all fleeting moments, no longer than a word or a chord, and they are slight integrations. They are, however, not to be slighted, because *Ulysses* is made of such small meanings. Speaking of the overall organization of the last chapters of the novel, Ellmann notes that "in the temporary union of the two [i.e., Stephen and Bloom] Joyce affirms his perception of community."[12] Joyce affirms this perception as well by means of the language. The text of *Ulysses*, according to Jack P. Dalton, contained an even greater emphasis on language as a unifying element of human relations. Dalton discusses how "a number of Joyce's special effects have been trivialized out of the text" by misled printers. Among many examples, he cites "that part of 'Circe' where Bella becomes a man and Bloom a woman and Bello . . . invites bidders to 'examine shis points. Handle hrim,' 'shis' and 'hrim' being amalgrams of the masculine and feminine pronouns."[13] The amalgrams unify persons by joining parts of pronouns and, were they restored to the text, would act as additional evidence of Joyce's interest in symbolizing community through language. Patterns are seen to work here for the integration and relation of the diverse material, building a form of community.

It is, of course, a community whose social contract is only the rules of grammar, and only by means of analogy can the structures of one replicate the structures of the other. (Although if Joyce felt, as has been shown, that biology and grammar are analogous, the connection between sociology and grammar can be no less possible.) The fragility of a communal organization built of language-parts lies precisely in the substitutability of those parts. The masculine pronoun to Molly is clearly only a marker of gender, not personality, as Bloom and Mulvey are both blended by a single signal: "How he kissed me under the Moorish wall . . . and then I asked him" (783). Bloom too acutely feels his precarious position in Molly's affection when he remembers how Boylan literally took both his grammatical and physical place: "She was humming. . . .

65

He other side of her. Elbow, arm. He" (167). Yet even in the degree of substitution the pronouns affirm the connections between people: when one acts, another somewhere must feel the effect, be replaced. What culture and history, religion and politics, or lust try to prevent, language tries to make possible. Social forms may be fragmented, individuals easily displaced, but language in its patterns works for a whole, bringing together at the level of the sentence (at least) what life sunders.

Yet, for all these vivid mimetic qualities of language's ordering—for all the realistic portrayal of physical aspects of life and society—the ordered patterns are restricted by the nature of their form; when Joyce's language treats something through the patterns at its disposal, it can represent only corresponding patterns in its subject. It cannot represent qualities other than those with pattern and system. The emphasis only on certain aspects to the exclusion of others is similar to Bloom's thought about the heart: "Seat of the affections . . . a pump after all." He quickly passes over the emotional to stress the mechanical and ordered. From this standpoint, the mechanical elements inherent in the patterns of language begin to take prominence, to stress only structures, and consequently to stress the merely physical reality which those structures represent.

The purely physical activity of sex lends itself readily to such a sense of the patterned mechanics of syntactic order. This description of adultery uses both diction and word order to stress an automatic character: "Of a bodily and mental male organism specially adapted for the superincumbent posture of energetic human copulation and energetic piston and cylinder movement necessary for the

66

complete satisfaction of a constant but not acute concu-
piscence resident in a bodily and mental female organism,
passive but not obtuse" (732). Phrases like "adapted for,"
"necessary for," included in a long run-on single phrase—
not even a sentence—give an air of inevitability and irrevocability which combines with the exactitude of the technical; they give a sense of the tired repetition of "love's
old sweet song." Here the limits of patterns in language
begin to show. The connections, interrelations and balance
which were observed in the earlier mimetic examples of
sex are here noticeably absent (except perhaps for the
word-pair *energetic/passive*, which is hardly supported by
a syntactic parallelism); only the technical aspect is important. A gap begins to appear between the event and the
language which enacts it, here working to the reduction
of the event by not stressing certain valuable and valid
characteristics, only reductive and mechanical ones. Compare Bloom's statement "Man and woman, love, what is
it? A cork and bottle" (499).

The patterns appear increasingly arbitrary as the dispro-
portion increases between structure and subject; they take
on a prominence which in turn aggravates the discrepancy.
Rather than present a subject, or enact it, they substitute
for it, take its place. When this occurs, the patterns become
empty; no longer mimetic and vivid, they appear to be
mere mechanics and idle repetition. Little is left in the
following sentence of the ability of the language to represent vividly the interrelationship of affection: "Love loves
to love love" (333). Stressing only pattern, such sentences
seem to stress their arbitrary nature as patterns.

Sex is a process "as natural as any and every natural act
of nature expressed or understood executed in natured na-

ture by natural creatures in accordance with . . . their natured natures" (733), as "Ithaca" intones with studied systemic stress. Yet the sentence itself is mere patterning, and as such appears to exclude the areas outside of nature and body, areas other than those circumscribed by orders. "Ithaca" is a chapter which tries most precisely to fix the physical world into an ordered system of question and response; it is there that the greatest number of seemingly arbitrary and mechanical language patterns betray the gap between themselves and their subject.

Trying in the very beginning to discuss Bloom's early life, in which he held nocturnal discussions similar to the one he then conducts with Stephen, the narrator asks in what ways Bloom's social life has developed. The answer: "From inexistence to existence he came to many and was as one received: existence to existence he was with any as any with any: from existence to nonexistence gone he would be by all as none perceived" (667–68). Here Bloom is surrounded by those members of society signified by the various pronouns; yet specific connections fail to materialize precisely because so many potential ones exist in one span. As the chapter progresses, the language becomes more and more mere patterning. It plays with the basic ordering and forming principles of words (described earlier), but here as if by way of avoiding an evaluation or elevation of its subject; Bloom shaving is described as follows: "with thought of aught he sought though fraught with nought" (674). Edward Lear could hardly be so melodiously nonsensical. Bloom is depicted as being so balanced and even as to seem to have no character at all: having a "masculine feminine passive active hand" (674).

This question on an important point (the meeting and

communication of Stephen and Bloom) and its answer
break down under the sheer accumulation of sentence
form:

> What, reduced to their simplest reciprocal form,
> were Bloom's thoughts about Stephen's thoughts about
> Bloom and Bloom's thoughts about Stephen's thoughts
> about Bloom's thoughts about Stephen?
> He thought that he thought that he was a jew
> whereas he knew that he knew that he knew that he
> was not. (682)

As the text moves typographically to its final egg-period,
the language takes on infinite negativity. Bloom shrinks as
the universe expands to such phrases as "nought nowhere
was never reached" (699) and "the departed [would] never
nowhere nohow reappear" (727). The technique of the
"Ithaca" chapter is too transparent in its relentless deflation and linguistic mechanism (even the question and answer form is contrived in the extreme) not to be reductive
in intention. By trying with the greatest detail to describe
the physical world (the flow of water for Bloom's cocoa or
the list of his possessions) and to do it through evidently
highly patterned and ordered language which deflates that
world, Joyce hints none too subtly both at the confines of
the physical and the limits of that part of language which
corresponds to it.

The unions of social structure symbolized by the patterns of language are likewise limited and restricted. There
is the hint of mere grammatical declension in the unions
affected by language; the "I you he they" seems an automatic running through of the grammatical patterns of
persons. (And *Moby-Dick*'s Pip appears here to read the
doubloon with his own *Murray's Grammar*.) One finds sen-

tences of repetition and insistence: "Look: look, look, look, look, look: you look at us" (282). Additionally there is the suggestion of arbitrariness in these patterns. No longer functional, they lose their usefulness in the world of the characters and are made to seem capriciously ordered. Joyce emphasizes the inherent implications of his syntactic order: its arbitrary and mechanical nature.

This drift into apparently mere patterning and mechanics and this emphasis on the purely physical represented by these patterns are very evident throughout the language of the novel. Even Bloom is described in a way that reduces him to the functions of his limbs and dismembers his humanity. We are told that he "inserted his hand mechanically into the back pocket of his trousers to obtain his latchkey" (668) or was "mechanically caressing" a whore (477). The activities of the body are stressed by the patterns of the language to such an extent that Bloom appears fragmented, alive only in his moving parts, almost a passive object: "His hand took his hat from the peg" (56); "His hand accepted the moist tender [pork kidney]" (60); "His slow feet walked him riverward" (151).

The dialectic which animates Joyce's art is one that counterbalances the spiritual with the physical, and the expressive form of the syntax enacts both terms of that dialectic. Throughout the discussion above, the physical part of the dialectic has been enacted for the characters by the patterns of language; yet in this fact lies another of the many paradoxes found in Joyce. The body, in physical existence, is generally supposed to individuate; it is the particular manifestation of a person. However, the physical representation of the characters in the novel loses its quality of specificity and individuation because it is expressed

PATTERNS

by the systemic in language: by patterns of verbs, by com-
binations of pronouns. That system, as part of the order of
language, is not specific or individual, but rather universal
and general. Precisely where the characters ought to appear most particularly—in their daily physical life—they
begin to be subsumed into abstraction and an order which
is, in their terms, capricious and limiting.

There is then another variable among the terms of
Joyce's dialectic within the expressive form of syntax. Along
with the pairs spirit / matter or mind / body there can
be the additional one of specific / general or individual /
patterned. While the language enacts the anticipated specificity of the character's individual physical and material
reality, it does so in terms of the language's own general
patterns and system and so ironically undoes that very
specificity. Thus the patterns are both useful and arbitrary
at the same time; they are creative yet restrictive of what
they create. At the level of the characters, the body is created and yet not allowed to individuate. This granted, it
can be seen that if characters are diminished in the novel,
this is due less to the aggrandizing of the text with largely
irrelevant material than to the dialectic within Joyce's
language, where the terms present the characters in often
contradictory ways.

Language represents the connections and relations for
the characters; yet these relations begin to take on a predictable course because the order of syntax which creates
them is itself programmatic. The patterns of language,
when separated from the subjects they can best enact,
seem to take on their own regulation according to their
syntax. Wittgenstein, trying to consider the way in which
sentences develop their sense, was once moved to suggest

71

by way of analogy a calculus of language: "Welche Rolle
der Satz in Kalkül spielt, das ist sein Sinn"; "eine allge-
meine Satzform bestimmt den Satz als Glied eines Kal-
küls."[14] ("Whatever function the sentence plays in a
calculus, that is its meaning;" "a general sentence form
determines the sentence as does a term in a calculus.") A
calculus, of course, is a system whereby a missing value
can be found by using the other existing parts. One notes
in passing Joyce's own calculus problem which appears in
the highly patterned "Ithaca": "A 4th typewritten letter
received by Henry Flower (let H. F. be L. B.) from Martha
Clifford (find M. C.)" (722). The mechanisms of language,
through the automatic patterns of syntax, seem to move
toward such a system. The repetitions of patterns stress
increasingly the nature of their own predictability; everything both in language and the life in the text represented
by that language seems to be predictable, a tired chorus
of love's old sweet song. Bloom feels this deadening repetition when he comments on cycles of stars and universes:
"Same old dingdong always." Life flows in a pattern as
monotonous as the language used to describe it: "Cityful
passing away, other cityful coming, passing away too:
other coming on, passing on" (164). Bloom's final recognition balances patterns so perfectly as to amount to nothing:
"No one is anything." All patterns in life and language are
orders, but they are occasionally so recognizably predictable as to be monotonous and mechanical.

Joyce lets this tendency to predictability and mechanical
repetition in language run its course, play out its full implications. In so doing, he makes clear all the inherent
limits to the physical life which the language enacts for
the characters in the novel. Particular physical existence

is mechanical; it appears to run automatically in patterns, and those patterns seem to have a repetitious familiarity. Joyce represents physical life most vividly, pays tribute to it, gives it frank expression; by means of language he imitates physical life. Yet also by means of his language he can show its limits and deflate its importance. Through the created language he can put the physical component of the life of the novel into some perspective.

A sense of reduction is a desirable effect in many ways, providing a much needed deflation to the easily overemphasized pathos of Bloom's adultery. "Ithaca" tartly points out the "inanity of extolling virtue" (734), and a necessary reevaluation of sex does much to shift the importance away from Bloom's pathetic side and onto his more adaptable and lasting virtues. The necessary reevaluation is carried out by the language. On the beach at dusk, having responded to the uncovered charms of Gerty MacDowell, Bloom thinks about his wife and Boylan: "O, he did. Into her. She did. Done" (370). Here the fact of adultery is presented in its most elemental form (and, it is important to note, presented by Bloom himself in a chapter whose technique involves effusive romanticism). The simple verbs of activity, inexactly suggesting mere energy; a change in tense and time (*did* to *done*); an indication of direction through the often-used preposition and pronoun: these all combine to define the act as mere motion in space and time, the most minimal specifications of existence.

There is a need for this deflation; it is important to be able to take the view that there is much in physical life which is mechanical and, in one light, almost automatic. The language is allowed to display its mechanics and to stress them because the life it depicts is often mechanical and capricious. Seen in this perspective, life has its moments of mere movement, extension in space and time. Bloom's sudden revolting vision of men eating in the Burton restaurant is an instance of this perspective, and it is the ability to see in this way that redeems Bloom from the common horde. Stephen also takes this perspective when, for example, he thinks of sex as arbitrary: "clasped and sundered, did the coupler's will" (38). In a similar manner the language's ability to render what is mechanical as such gives it a quality of higher vision.

This higher vision is a recognition of the limits of the physical world of the novel. The dimension of the physical is important: digestion and gestation are important natural processes, fundamental to life. By no means are they to be shunned or neglected, but rather given their full honest expression in mimetic language. Yet neither are such processes and the physicality of life to be overrated; important as they are, they are not the sum of man's existence nor of reality. There is much in the physical that is mechanical and repetitious, automatic and even demeaning: this is a significant point to be made about a book that was once considered obscene. The language suggests that there is more to life than adultery, or eating; it suggests further that the characters' lives have dimensions other than the physical.

In this higher vision Joyce demonstrates something else as well. Joyce's art was described earlier as consisting of the interaction of the inner world with the outer world, of the soul and reality, not only for the characters but also for the artist-figure; and that the dialectic was further complicated in its opposition by occurring in these two contrasting contexts. Thus it is only from one perspective that these

74

patterns of language are so limiting and arbitrary: the perspective of the characters. In showing the limits of the reality of physical experience for the characters in the novel, what Joyce is demonstrating—and paradoxically—is the creativity of the intellect at the level of the artist.

It is the nature of physical life to take patterns, but it is the nature of mind to use them. The language which in one context recognizes limits of the physical world in those patterns, only stresses the limitless potentiality for using those patterns in creative activity in another. The order that seems dictated for the characters in their world of the novel is indeed dictated, but by the artist; what is arbitrary for them is what he thinks and makes appropriate. What is capricious and mechanical for the characters (language reducing sex to a machinelike movement, for example), through the agency of the very patterns of language that make it so, comes to illustrate the creative intellect of the artist who uses and creates with those patterns to such effect. Every physical restriction in the world of the novel only reflects the freedom and license of the artistic mind which imposes it.

Joyce is interested in all patterns because they are appropriate, expressive, and effective. The patterns in language provide for the characters (at their level) the reality of the physical world; for the artist they provide the schemes and systems with which he exercises his artistic intelligence, ranking and apportioning, ordering his world of art. All the contrivance in *Ulysses,* from schemes to syntax but especially in syntax, illustrates the powers of creative intelligence. The artist orders in patterns not only the work itself, but also his language and the reality of the world of the novel created by that language.

We are in for a sequentiality of improbable possibles though possibly nobody after having grubbed up a lock of cwold cworn aboove his subject probably in Harrystotalies or the vivle will go out of his way to applaud him on the onboiassed back of his remark for utterly impossible as are all these events they are probably as like those which may have taken place as any others which never took person at all are ever likely to be.

Finnegans Wake

4 Potential Order as Entelechy

The sentences examined in the previous chapter, fixed by the patterns of language and held in control by the over-arching order of syntax, seem to be all of a piece, complete in and of themselves. The various requirements of grammar are met, occasionally by some restless meandering of the phrases, often by rigid adherence to apparently me-chanical patterns. By the end of the sentences, verbs have subjects and predicates, adjectives and pronouns have referents. There is the suggestion that each sentence final-ly fulfills the grammatical requirements set up by its own different parts, that it moves onward, in a devolving alter-nation of phrases, like the Liffey to the sea, and that this movement culminates in a particular end, the sentence realized as a finished whole in all its patterns. "John Henry Menton, filling the doorway of Commercial Buildings, stared from winebig oyster eyes, holding a fat gold hunter watch not looked at in his fat left hand not feeling it" (253). This sentence seems pushed on and on by the string of phrases. The two adjective phrases at the end ("not looked at," "not feeling") separated by a prepositional phrase, are compressed from possible longer subordinate clauses to give a greater sense of movement.[1] Although they seem strung out like beads on a string, by the end of the sentence they clearly refer anaphorically to their referents, *watch* and *hand,* and they unite the sentence by subtly suggesting the various subjects of their verbs: Menton not looking, he—or his hand—not feeling. The strung-out looseness of alternating phrases has in the end moved to a grammatically tightened whole. As Lindley Murray says, syntax makes a complete sense; and order has its creative potential.

Yet order and completion are conditions not always fully met, and if the reader of *Ulysses* is struck by the appropriate order of sentences he is no less struck by the prevalence of non-sentences or incomplete ones. "Invent a story for some proverb which?" (69); "the lovely name you" (285); "I couldn't do" (266); "Wish I could" (289): while the fragmentation of syntax here is caused in the first part by the associative leaps of the interior monologue, its effect is due also to the fact that the disruption seems to run counter to the orderly connection syntax has established. "A raindrop spat on his hat. He drew back and saw an instant of shower spray dots over the grey flags. . . . I thought it would" (90). There is a gap in this last sentence, albeit a small one; it is a lacuna which somehow must be filled. What should come in this particular case lies already in the surrounding context: the word-pattern of *raindrop* and *dot* (as verb) readily suggests *rain* for the missing link. The separation of sentences, or even of words themselves, is often bridged by the weight of cliché; "Good fit for a" (271); "Pin cuts lo" (twice—168, 263). In another unfinished example there is more missing: 'Those literary etherial people they are all. Dreamy, cloudy, symbolistic" (166).

The sentence here makes a full stop, but what follows immediately are the words in the gap. The period is not the end of the first sentence, nor do the succeeding words make another sentence; there are connections of syntax which draw the two together.

More than the immediate context or cliché then, there are the patterns of language themselves which indicate what the missing part is. Paradoxically, but not unexpectedly, sentences that appear not to fulfill the order of syntax only end up asserting it: the syntax evokes the order it seems to revoke. The order of Joyce's sentences accommodates the disjunction and fragmentation by suggesting what the sentence does not complete; as Roland Barthes observes, "Language, as sentence, period and paragraph superimposes on these discontinuous categories existing at the level of discourse the appearance of continuity. Because no matter how discontinuous language itself may appear, its structure is so well established in the experience of each man that he grasps discourse as a continuous reality." Barthes refers here to spoken language, but he goes on to claim that written language also contains this continuity by means of imposed order; he notes that written sentences are marked by "a constraint, an obligatory rubric: the completed sentence."[2] Joyce points to this obligatory order of the completed sentence by his fragmentation of that order and, consequently, by the very fragmentation, emphasizes as well the continuity of language in the appropriate form of its potential order.

The adjective in the following example readily indicates the unprovided predicate adjective which is required by the last verb: "They want special dishes to pretend they're" (175). Similarly the verb in one tense, *blew*, suggests the one missing, *blow:* "Sheet of music blew out of my hand against the high school railings. Luckily it didn't" (156). In the similar examples following, the requirements of syntax dictate what the movement of the sentence should supply, specifically an infinitive verb: "Petals too tired to" (71); "Wonder if he's too far to" (367); "Always build one door opposite another for the wind to" (117). In much the same manner, but at a greater length, the correct order and pattern which are the necessity of syntax suggest a subordinate clause ("if not . . . then") to follow Stephen's thought: "And yet it was in some way if not as memory fabled it" (24). Other examples present an incompleteness whose final order is to be determined by the subordination of relative adjective clauses: "You will see who" (47), "Once knew a gentleman who" (371); or the subordination of time: "Hate company when you" (73), "Suppose she was gone when he" (653), "Just when I" (180), "Music I often thought when she" (282); or cause: "Because you never know exac" (288). Here again the dictates of syntax provide the missing part, filling out the incomplete sentence: "Also. . . . Yes. I. Do it in the bath. Curious longing I" (85). The last phrase requires a verb; it must be transitive, in the first person singular. It is adumbrated if not given. Similarly, one finds "Why did she me?" (275). The rhyme of the two pronouns has a music of its own; and Stuart Gilbert explains that such examples where the central verb is omitted are the equivalent of the musical hollow fifth.[3] While that may be true of this latter example, from "Sirens," it is hardly true of the former, from "Lotus Eaters." Musical forms do not fill the gaps in the sentences, but the syntactic forms do, bridging subject and object. The voids in the sentences where the rhythm seems to stop are filled in and moved onward by the requirements of syntax. Directed and channelled by patterns of language to ends dictated by the existing sentence-parts, the fragmented phrases are made to seem whole. Motion and syntactic order bring into being the final sentence which lies potentially in the parts.

In this Joyce is extending and exploiting the consequences of the order of syntax. The previous chapter demonstrated that he uses the patterns of language to emulate the corresponding patterns in life; those structures were highly mimetic, although the patterns had the tendency to turn predictably repetitious and limited. In this chapter it will be shown how Joyce pursues further the effect of the order of language's expressive form; he lets the language play out, as it were, along those very lines and patterns, allowing it to develop a movement directed by its order.

In the movement towards the completion of the sentence by the parts within it, the structural rhythm—as the flow and pull of the incomplete sentences can be called— is maintained even beyond the sentence line. The interrelation of rhythm, structure, and final form was noted by Joyce as early as his Paris thoughts on aesthetics: "Rhythm seems to be the first or formal relation of part to part in any whole or of a whole to its parts, or of any part to the whole of which it is a part. . . . Parts constitute a whole as far as they have a common end." (25 March 1903, Paris). (Joyce never wrote a better analysis of his own style.) The emphasis on form and on the parts contributing to a finished piece is indeed the principle of the sentences: their grammatical parts have the common end in the fulfillment of syntactical requirements, and the end of the sentence (not the typographical end, but the grammatical end) is achieved by the motion of the phrases in rhythmic balance. Joyce, through Stephen, calls this structural rhythm the "first entelechy" (432); and it is through a consideration of this clearly Aristotelian term that one can recognize a fundamental concept at work in Joyce's emphatic use of the patterns in language: he has further ideas for making his order appropriate.

It would not be necessary to read far into Aristotle, probably not as far as Joyce himself, to find these notions of movement and completion (and to be struck by the similarities in terminology between them and Joyce's language). *Entelechy* was for Aristotle the fulfillment of possibilities inherent in matter by the action of form, a realization that was achieved by the kinetic process of movement: "The fulfillment of what exists potentially . . . is motion." The motion brings about an actualization of those parts which are potentially the final product; as the word *entelechy* implies—*en* and *telos*—matter contains its ends within itself. These ends then "by a continuous movement originated by an internal principle, arrive at some completion."[4] Aristotle explains most succinctly: "Everything that comes to be moves towards a principle, i.e. an end . . . and the actuality is the end, and it is for the sake of this that the [movement] is acquired. . . . Further, matter exists in a potential state, just because it may come to form; and when it exists *actually*, then it is in its form."[5] The realization of formal possibilities inherent in matter by the action of movement—one could hardly ask for a better definition of the effect of the particular half-finished sentences: for *form* read the order required by syntactic patterns, an order that operates on the few but potentially meaningful syntactic units which make up the phrases, and that, by the dynamic movement of the unfolding language, brings out the final form potential in the syntax of those phrases. The sentence-parts bring with them the seeds of their own fruition, and the motion of the sentence to the actualization of the syntactic form inherent in it is the self-realization of those lexical possibilities.

Aristotle speaks of geometry in terms equally applicable to grammar: "Potentially existing constructions are discovered by being brought to actuality."[6] The potential sentences which are imbedded within patterns of language and grammatical parts are brought into being and structured into syntactical form by the sentence's movement; and an incomplete sentence only makes this potential emergence more evident. "I think she knew by the way she" (155). The missing end of this abrupt sentence is brought out by what is already part of the sentence. The end must have a verb (alone or part of a verb phrase); that verb must be in the third person singular; it must be in the past; the manner of its action is indicated ("by the way she"): part of speech, person, tense are all determined by what has gone before. What the existing parts require will come to be the final part of the sentence. Joyce exploits syntax in such a way as to anticipate an end to the movement and to indicate that end through the pattern of the parts.

To bring idea and example close together, take the following sentence where entelechy is mentioned explicitly. Stephen thinks: "But I, entelechy, form of forms, am I by memory because under everchanging forms" (189). Again an incomplete sentence, the balance of "I . . . am I . . . because" sets up the order of what the sentence must be. The "everchanging forms" must be amplified by something in a following clause (Stephen is Stephen because, despite ever changing forms, his soul remains the same). The entelechy of language's patterned form, as well as that of life's, keeps him to that.

As seen by this last quotation, the concept of entelechy is by no means foreign to the novel as a theme. It will be helpful in understanding its applicability to Joyce's prose to consider how this concept is discussed in the text, as it presents a view of Aristotle quite different from the familiar definitions found in the *Notebooks* and the *Portrait*. Stephen articulates the notions of becoming and self-fulfillment several times early in the day, and he has much recourse to them in his debate in the library. At Deasy's school, caught up in the rote teaching of faded lessons of history, Stephen ponders: "It must be a movement then, an actuality of the possible as possible. Aristotle's phrase formed itself. . . . The soul is in a manner all that is: the soul is the form of forms" (25–26). The motion of things which come to pass in the flow of history, as Stephen tries to understand it, only follows the patterns delineated by Artistotle of bringing potentiality into actuality. For Stephen, the growth of life, historical or personal, is an entelechic process. By bringing up the last phrase about the soul, Stephen shows that he is interested in the implications of entelechy as progress: "form of forms" refers to another, related idea of Aristotle. While the motion of potentia is primarily physical, for which reason Aristotle articulated it in the *Physics*, the soul as the form of forms, the highest end of the body, comes from the *Metaphysics*.[7] In bringing these two related ideas of Aristotle together, Stephen effects a very subtle and imporant shift in emphasis from mere motion to progression. He has done in

83

the span of a sentence what Aristotle does carefully in the course of his works. From the idea of physical motion Aristotle develops the sense of a purposive end to that motion; the change lifts his thinking from the physical plane to the metaphysical. Werner Jaeger considers the drift of Aristotle's thought (and, incidentally, the shift in Stephen's thinking):

> Metaphysics is based on physics according to Aristotle in the first place because it is nothing but the conceptually necessary completion of the experimentally revealed system of moving nature. . . .
> With reference to motion the form is the entelechy inasmuch as in its form each thing possesses the end of motion realized within itself. . . . Locomotion serves the special laws of organic coming-to-be and passing-away, which in their turn depend on form. The entelechy of beings that come to be and pass away is the height of this organic development.
> . . . In every kind of motion Aristotle's gaze is fastened on the end . . . that something fixed and normative is making its way into existence—the form.[8]

Growth and progress continue to interest Stephen because, as a young man, he faces a future which asks him to grow and mature into the artist he feels is within him. Entelechy for Stephen seems to offer the affirmation of his life. On the beach, after his experiments with the sensible things of sight and space, he follows up his earlier Aristotelian musings: "My soul walks with me, form of forms" (44); "I throw this ended shadow from me, manshape ineluctable, call it back. Endless, would it be mine, form of my form?" (48). His shadow, which leads him through his walk on the beach and is the manifestation of his physical matter, he transforms, as is fitting in the protean chapter, into the metaphysical end and fulfillment of that physical body.

In the library discussion of Shakespeare's life and art Stephen uses his ideas of Aristotle to the utmost. He prepares for dialectic and debate by beginning to "unsheathe [his] dagger definitions. Horseness is the whatness of all-horse" (186). Some reflection on "Aristotle's experiment [that] necessity is that in virtue of which it is impossible that one can be otherwise" (192) diverts his attention from the discussion between Best and Eglinton of the group of young poets from which Stephen knows himself to be excluded. Taunts and disagreement from the oracular Æ go unanswered, as Stephen reflects on his debt to Russell of five pounds. He tries mentally to disavow the debt: "Wait. Five months. Molecules all change. I am other I now" (189). But he cannot follow this adopted materialist line of thought. His Aristotelianism brings him back, and he refers once more to the final realization of himself, his soul (in a sentence which, as was seen, is itself entelechic): "But I, entelechy, form of forms, am I by memory because under everchanging forms" (189). His self, which is the possibility inherent in him, comes to realization through the movement of time and does not make him another: "that which I was is that which I am and that which in possibility I may come to be" (194). He cannot shake loose from his debt, for he only becomes himself through time.

While this fact may be difficult for debtors, this inability to escape what is oneself, it becomes the sine qua non of the artist. According to Stephen, Shakespeare as an artist finds and makes himself in the world outside: "He found in the world without as actual what was in his world within as possible" (213); the life he lived and the works he wrote are

85

the realizations of what lay within him. What Maeterlinck expresses in his dictum that *"if Socrates leave his house today he will find the sage seated on his doorstep,"* Stephen succinctly calls a "meeting [of] ourselves": "Every life is many days, day after day. We walk through ourselves" (213). A motion outward, the progress to some goal in space and time, finally brings one to what lay potentially within. This movement is explicitly mentioned in the *Portrait*, in the beginning of the passage so important to our understanding the dialectic in Joyce's art and language: "I go to encounter for the millionth time the reality of experience and to forge in the smithy of my soul the uncreated conscience of my race" (253). This statement of Stephen's aesthetic credo clearly stresses an active movement, and it also suggests why he is so concerned with the possibilities of his own development. Both life and art consist of motion outward to find and to work with what lies deepest within. The Shakespeare who went to London, according to Stephen, found in his plays only what he seemingly left in Stratford; and the Joyce who fled Dublin did so only to return to it in art. Aristotle would say, and Stephen would agree, that the artist through his art brings to fulfillment what lay inherent in his materials; only Stephen (and Joyce) would add that his material is not like the sculptor's, the physical matter of stone and wood, but the physical matter which is his own life and his own language.

Even gone in his cups at night in the brothel, Stephen adheres to this theory of becoming; he states clearly enough: "What went forth to the ends of the world to traverse not itself. God, the sun, Shakespeare, a commercial traveller, having itself traversed in reality itself, becomes that self. . . . Self which it itself was ineluctably preconditioned to become" (505). This is a strange crew who journey to find what lies potentially in themselves. The sun moves from its nativity to its decline; it is the sun which casts Stephen's shadow on the beach. Shakespeare, according to Stephen's theory, is of course in this company. Even Bloom is not excluded from the list of entelechic luminaries; his journey from home at morning and back at night, trying vainly in-between to canvass an ad, is the same as Shakespeare's to London or the sun's to the west, no different and no less important (the more so that a book has been written about that self-fulfilling odyssey). God, the Creator, belongs as is His right as the begetter of Himself and all things.

What has been discussed above as being a thematic notion has earlier been demonstrated as being syntactical: the motion of sentences to complete the syntactic ends within them is an entelechy of language unique with Joyce. Although priding himself on being an Aristotelian—he claimed in his poem "The Holy Office" to bring "the mind of witty Aristotle" to the drab life of the Dublin of his youth—Joyce's interest in Aristotle was not thorough; much like his theory of aesthetics in the *Portrait*, "applied Aquinas," his use of the idea of entelechy is applied Aristotle. It was the system of ideas in Aristotle which appealed to Joyce both as model and method for the artist. Aristotle's clear organization and ordering of large bodies of material could not but be attractive to the planner in Joyce. Joyce's Aristotelianism was fundamentally creative; it provided him with concepts and ideas he could recast in the smithy of his soul to forge his own language and his art. He applied his own notion of a linguistic entelechy because it enabled him to construct a framework for the creativity of his style in its patterns. The appropriate order of his words on the page has several far-reaching effects. In commenting on the discussion of appropriate order, Budgen claimed to be impressed by the sense the words gave him "that a new province of material had been found."[9] That new province was not only the epic form and the monologue technique of the novel (as Budgen realized), but also that of a new province of language where the expressive form of appropriate order takes on new directions.

The entelechy of syntax takes the order of words in the sentence one step further. The mechanics described in the previous chapter are like the basic parts of Aristotle's thought, concerned with physical aspects: the constructs of the patterning mimetically recreate the physical mechanics with which Nature is replete. One critic claims that in *Ulysses* the words and techniques come between the reader and the action,[10] but it can be seen that this is hardly so; imitating Nature, language is itself an action. Yet the last chapter also showed that there were limitations to the patterned and physical dimension of Joyce's language, limitations largely in terms of repetition and reduction.

In a way related to the limits of the physical dimension, the patterns inherent in language are also limited by their association with spatiality. Benjamin Lee Whorf, through his work with languages other than those of Indo-European origin, was able to see in what ways western languages shape the world they describe. He notes something of particular importance here, that English is characterized by a syntax whose patterns blend components together in a "mechanical mixture." The blending of components by mere addition (his example is *spotted* + *cat* = "spotted cat") takes on a particular implication; the blend-

88

ing and the division of sentences into subject and predicate (another mixture) have led, in Whorf's words, to "the philosophical and also naive notion of an actor who produces an action." (A similar judgment could be made on the division into action and object or prepositional phrase and object, constructions that have been prominent in the examples of the expressive form of the physical.) Whorf continues: "The mechanistic way of thinking is perhaps just a type of syntax natural . . . to western Indo-European languages, rigidified and intensified by Aristotle and the latter's medieval and modern followers." Of essential importance is the philosophical cast of English as Whorf sees it: "[English] has analyzed reality largely in terms of what it calls 'things' (bodies and quasibodies) plus modes of extensional but formless existence that it calls 'substances' or 'matter.' It tends to see existence through a binomial formula that expresses any existent as a spatial form plus a spatial formless continuum related to the form. . . . Nonspatial existents are imaginatively spatialized and charged with similar implications of form and continuum." He also notes that English tends toward "imaginatively spatializing qualities and potentials that are quite nonspatial."[11]

Thus the limits imposed by the order of language and the restrictions of its patterns can be measured not only in terms of the inherent physical mimesis of its construction, but also in terms of its inherent spatiality. The result is an elevation of the dimension of space over that of time, and a conflation of both. There are many points in *Ulysses* where this metaphysical conflation is mentioned. Stephen's thinking in the "Proteus" chapter begins with a discussion of the properties of things, as if he, and not Aristotle, were the subject of Whorf's comment above: "Limits of the diaphane. But he adds: in bodies. Then he was aware of them bodies before of them coloured" (37). Stephen discusses the concepts of *neben-* and *nacheinander,* which Joyce called his own definitions of space and time,[12] and he considers a "very short space of time through very short times of space" (37). Here he is clearly and consciously mixing the two entities. Later, in "Scylla," he talks of his fate: "that lies in space which I in time must come to, ineluctably" (217). He plays with the word *time* in the sense of chronology and of the temporal nature of things. As the book moves to the end of a long day, the conflation becomes even more pronounced. Stephen may have been aware of the ambivalence of his terms, but the tired narrator of "Eumaeus" heaps cliché on cliché in confusing them; he speaks of a "lengthy space of time" and "heaps of time" (664). An answer in "Ithaca" ponders the tension between the two dimensions: "An unsatisfactory equation between an exodus and return in time through reversible space and an exodus and return in space through irreversible time" (728).

This last description is also a statement of the condition of the entire novel. The direction of its conflation is to stress the spatiality of time; the sentence above is itself spatial, as its syntax makes it reversible in place. The novel articulates the concept of time in terms the order of language can articulate; as Whorf notes, the mechanical mixture of English expresses time in terms of field and extension. Granting that notion, temporality is presented only obliquely, not in its own terms, by ordered elements which stress spatiality. It is no surprise to find the great limits, orders, and plans in *Ulysses* as those plotted in space. The many contrivances of near-misses and meetings, crossing paths and patterns in the construction of plot are charted in space, written with the map. The labyrinth is the form of order, and it is a spatial puzzle. The attempt to plan out a day in Dublin by means of moving through the city in space is the most fundamental example of this conflation of dimensions. The schemes of organs is an attempt by objects to make physical what is supposed, in the end, to combine into something temporal. The organs per chapter add up neither to a full man nor to an endless, timeless day. It is the province of *Finnegans Wake* to do that. Because of the strong reliance in *Ulysses* on the paterns of language, patterns which give meaning and order in spatial ways, the novel runs into a conflict trying to be temporal.

Yet Joyce uses Aristotle, redeeming him from Whorf's harsh judgement, to provide a new dimension for his own style. The entelechic concept which Joyce develops in language in some measure obviates the limitations of spatiality; what it offers is an impulse beyond the linear order of the sentence. Any sentence on the page is a paradoxical entity. It occupies space, as it has extension and limit; its meaning, in some measure, is the effect of its entirety, the total of its parts. Yet a sentence is also read, its meaning unfolded in sequence, and thus it has a temporal quality. A sentence balances spatiality (*place* or *field* in Whorf's terms) and temporality (motion through its elements). What Joyce does by means of his syntactic entelechy, the developing of the sentence, is to gesture precisely to this latent temporal dimension.

As Aristotle shifts in his thought from physical motion to the process of progression and development, so Joyce, utilizing the same concept of a syntactic order as entelechy, moves his language from physical patterning into other dimensions. For Aristotle this was the change from the *Physica* to *De Anima;* for Joyce it was a change in emphasis from the mechanical patterns themselves to the moving progress within those patterns.[13] For both, this represented a change in dimension away from the motion and activity in physical space to the process of motion in time, from ordered spatiality to telic temporality. The entelechic sentences discussed here, while sharing the order of syntax with the patterned, physically representative sentences of chapter 3, go beyond them. The very progress of the sentence is a motion greater than mere miming of physical kinesis; the sentences to some extent create beyond themselves, beyond their physical presence. In suggesting their ends in, but beyond, themselves, what they can and will be, the entelechic sentences do what the merely mechanical ones could not; they break away from the restrictions of spatial and physical pattern and enter the realm of progression, of motion throughout time. As against the rigidly ordered dimension of space, the sentences suggest the longer and more fluid dimension of process in time.

Order, necessary connections, and the rigid patterning of pronouns and referents are clearly the focus of this example: "That was a tuningfork the tuner had that he forgot that he now struck" (264). This sentence is all closed up, complete, tightly connected, and whole: it is of a piece. A sentence which is entelechic, while being ordered by syntax, is more open, even simple and abrupt; it suggests that something is to come: "What perfume does your?" (85). A noun must follow and a transitive verb; all that can unfold is indicated. The sentence, through a dynamic movement channelled by its patterns of syntax, points to a progress, where it is to go. Similarly one finds "excites them when they're" (368). The following sentence has, as it were, a future before it: "Ireland was dedicated to it or whatever that" (113). Its parts indicate something into which it will develop; its potential is to be released in time. In these unfinished sentences one feels the impulse to what is beyond, with the order of syntax pointing the direction; and in sensing that, one senses the sentence line as developing and continuing temporal entity.

By making his sentences entelechic, structuring them so that their parts dictate what they must be and the dynamics of the sentence move toward that end, Joyce emphasizes the latent temporal dimension. All of these entelechic sentences will develop and project themselves into the void where they seem to stop; there is the expectation of something more to come, an anticipation. Stephen mentions an idea very close to this when he drunkenly considers his own impossible riddle of the fox and the grandmother: "Why striking eleven? Proparoxyton. Moment before the next Lessing says" (559). The reference to Lessing is apt; as noted, earlier in the day Stephen thought of his distinction of space and time as *neben-* and *nacheinander*. In the *Laokoön*, Lessing uses these terms as he discusses the difficulty for the poet to describe a continuum, to capture an *Augenblick*.[14] Joyce, by ordering his language in his particular way, by underscoring its devolving dynamics of patterns, begins to answer Lessing's problem, a problem faced by all verbal artists.

The subtle change in dimension by means of the language takes one a long way toward understanding some of the fundamentally original aspects of Joyce's creativity.

93

The movement away from the spatial extension of the sentence, by a particular emphasis on the patterns of language which determine what the sentence can and will be beyond the page, is a move toward a temporal dimension; it is there that Joyce can begin to break the bonds of the written line. A. Walton Litz, in his very astute reading of the development of Joyce's oeuvre, notes that the "work on *Ulysses* and *Finnegans Wake* is characterized by a growing conflict between his aesthetic ideal of 'simultaneity' and the consecutive nature of language." Litz remarks further that this dissatisfaction grew as the work progressed; "as *Ulysses* and *Finnegans Wake* developed Joyce moved further and further from the conventions of sequence and order established by traditional fiction."[15] What Litz does not recognize is that, in the particular twist Joyce gives his patterned language through the notion of a linguistic entelechy, he can move beyond the consecutive nature of the sentence on the page towards the simultaneity amid pattern he found so desirable in music.[16] Joyce wants to achieve a temporal order within language, but it is an order which is impossible. No amount of ingenuity in recreating the fugue form can compensate for the necessity of reading sequentially and orderly; no variety of overlapping harmonious voices in *Finnegans Wake* can actually overcome the requirements of reading word by word to "hear" those voices. Joyce certainly recognized the impossibility of attaining a real simultaneity in written art, but he achieves the next best thing: through the entelechy of his sentences he emphasizes as strongly as possible the temporal element embedded within language. Moreover, and true to the paradoxical in him, it is by stressing the *temporality* of language (its coming-to-be)

94

that Joyce approaches that "simultaneity" which one or-
dinarily associates with nontemporal art; by stressing the
chronology in the syntagmatic order, he reaches beyond
synchrony towards an achronology. Joyce has created a
language which, linearly half-done, can begin to project its
own future parts. With such a language, the songs and
resonant musicality of "Sirens" are plausible; they are part
of a language of duration in time. Moreover the reverber-
ating imagery of the myriad potential words in one printed
word of *Finnegans Wake,* words which leap beyond the
forms of sentence and book to suggest all that will be and
also all that was, is an obvious possibility, easily obtainable
for Joyce because of his language and indeed only a few
years away in time. The entelechy of appropriate order
gives the artist great freedom. The temporality of *Ulysses,*
its long June day, may be achieved less in its overt and
superficial order of hours and length of chapters, than in
the pending sense of coming-to-be that lies within its very
sentences. The formal patterns, as noted earlier, are inherently spatial—all of the structures are related to space; it is
in the progression of the ordered sentences coming to an
end that time is expressed.

With an entelechy of sentences, where, moving by their
own possibilities, they project their own final form in time,
there must be something that exists beyond both motion
and time, something which activates the sentences. To set
in motion and to use time are the powers of only one, select
entity. In the words of the Aristotelian critic A. E. Taylor,
one argues "from the continuity of motion to its depen-
dence on a source or sources which are permanent and
present throughout the whole everlasting world-process."[17]
For Aristotle, the end of the process of becoming outlined

in the *Metaphysics*, that unmoved last thing, is also the Prime Mover, God. In that Supreme One lay the first power to create form out of matter (and one can see how appealing Aristotle was to medieval thinkers on this point). Jaeger points out that even in the late draft of the *Metaphysics* Aristotle "made clever use of the conceptions of entelechy and actuality in attacking the problem of God."[18] Joyce does no less; changing world-process to word-process, and using a language which is entelechic and (even temporally) actualizing, he cleverly apotheosizes himself.

Young Stephen's statements to Lynch in chapter 4 of the *Portrait* are germane:

> The artist, like the God of creation, remains within or behind or beyond or above his handiwork, invisible, refined out of existence, indifferent, paring his finger-nails.
>
> —Trying to refine them also out of existence, said Lynch. (215)

Rather than consider this statement in terms of the more widely held idea of Flaubert,[19] one can view it in the light of Joyce's Aristotelianism. By that logic one need not see Joyce as essentially "indifferent." In terms of the artistic verbal entelechy, Joyce has a stake in the matter of his art; the notion from Aristotle is reapplied to magnify his kind of creative activity. Joyce does not see himself like God in creating from nothing; even Stephen is aware that he creates art from life, "from the sluggish matter of the earth" (*Portrait*, 169); and Aristotle would agree with Stephen's choice of terms. Rather, Joyce can consider himself "divine" by being the first and prime mover in a linguistic process which first enacts the physical and spatial and then suggests the temporal. Joyce creates particular structures of language with their certain tensions of pattern and order, and these structures continue beyond the words on the page. He begins the movement of the sentences; and through the dynamic evolvement of his language according to its syntactic laws, what he creates seems to exist separate from him.[20] This illusion of the self-sufficiency of words is carefully cultivated by Joyce; the disinterested artist is a useful pose. Yet in the very constructs of his language he reveals his own commitment to the most basic workings of his art, projecting into the void beyond the sentence, brooding over the abyss. The Holy Ghost did no more. Joyce's very language manifests him and reveals the kind of appropriate effort he exerts in his work. While the god may seem to be "invisible," his handiwork reveals him most clearly in the universal system he creates and sustains.

Thus entelechy and the temporality it evokes point us back to the level of the book on which we are primarily aware of patterns arranged by the creative mind of the artist-figure. In chapter 3 we noted that the physical world of mimetic patterns, in its limitations for the characters, served ultimately to demonstrate the active intelligence that ordered and created those patterns in language. The concept of the prime mover is another way of revealing the creative intelligence which motivates those patterns. By cultivating the notion of entelechy in the patterns of his syntax, Joyce tips his hand to reveal the guiding force of intelligence which at one level, that of the artist, starts and sustains the host of patterns and orders which, at the level of the characters in the text, enacts the physical world of being, motion, and time. It is through the entelechy of his sentences that Joyce lets the connection between the levels of character and artist be glimpsed: it is the chain of syntactic order which stretches from one sphere to the other, his language's great chain of being. That chain unites the creating of language with the reality created by it, binds the artist to his work, and binds the character to the artist.

The shift from spatial to temporal progression, while it provides the artist with his degree of creativity, has one final consequence. Because the expressive form of language influences the entire world of *Ulysses,* the entelechy of language at the level of the artist influences the "reality of experience" for the characters within the novel. As the sentences suggest their completion in time, they move from a merely linear, sequential notion of the order of words to a consequential one. When one part not only precedes the others but actually comes in some measure to dictate what they will be, it acts in some causal relationship with the other potential parts. The sentences progress to some end, but that end is determined by the rules of syntax. Thus there is a point where the processes of nature and the patterns of language which describe and enact them seem to take on a predictability in the world of the characters, that other context of language's dialectic.

Reading a letter from his daughter Milly, Bloom thinks poignantly of her growing independence and maturity. "A soft qualm regret, flowed down his backbone, increasing. Will happen, yes. Prevent. Useless: can't move. Girl's sweet light lips. Will happen too. . . . Useless to move now. Lips kissed, kissing kissed" (67). The reciprocal character of emotion, the balance of give and take expressively figured in language (as demonstrated in the previous chapter) becomes only a phrase in a natural process where things are determined to come to a certain end. The staccato alternation of the imperative *prevent* with the future tense *will happen* and the negative *can't* all give a sense of irrevocable direction in time. A few sentences earlier Bloom calls this "destiny" (66). Aristotle's view of life coming by necessity to what is within it and Joyce's language of stressed patterns are here united in a sense of determination: it is both anatomy and syntax as destiny.

It is precisely because the patterns of language, the connections and relations of the syntax, are themselves pre-established and determined that they make the developing language act as a seeming determiner for the life it represents. Joyce's entelechy of language, which is part of the order of syntax, is obliged to develop along the prescribed lines of syntax. As those patterns can often be repetitive, so the dynamic language which follows them consequently seems more and more determined, and the reality enacted for the characters by the expressive form seems analogously restricted and circumscribed. The repetitive patterns of language are seemingly raised by the movement of their entelechy to a determinative causality. By stressing the development of a sentence according to its syntactic rules, Joyce may emphasize the temporality of language at the level of the artist, but the consequence at the level of the characters is a sense of causality in their symbolically depicted lives.

The unfinished quality of sentences is quite often achieved by their interruption at a crucial syntactic juncture, frequently a temporal conjunction. All of the following sentences end with a marker of temporal condition: "Was he there when the father?" (103); "Saw his hair just when I" (260); "Music I often thought when she" (282);

"Suppose I when I was" (369). Slightly different in not ending with a temporal conjunction, the following nevertheless also suggests temporal condition: "Still I feel" (370). By ending at the point at which the syntax suggests temporal relations, the order of language which completes the sentences is stressed, but more pointedly a certain suggestion of causality is also indicated. Thus the causal connections which Bloom tries to make between the random events in his life are to some extent actualized by the causal relations between the entelechic parts in the expressive language used to describe those events. Bloom ponders as follows: "She didn't like [a dress] because I sprained my ankle first day she wore choir picnic at the Sugarloaf. As if that" (155). He neither proves nor disproves the reality of the connection, and the language he uses obviously denies any causal conditions. Nevertheless the *as if*, introducing a subordinate and conditional notion, and the *that*, referring back to the action, *sprained*, imply what would follow would have a mood and a subject; the determining sequence of the language rather strongly suggests the causal connection he tries to refute. In similar manner, but working more to his embarrassment and pain, Bloom ponders the phenomenon of his watch's stopping at 4:30: "Very strange about my watch. Wristwatches are always going wrong. Wonder is there any magnetic influence between the person because that was about the time he" (373). What Bloom considers primarily is the temporal connection between Boylan's visit to Molly and the stopping of the watch: "about the time he"; the syntax requires a temporal subordination. Yet Bloom indicates a causal connection: with his customary interest in pseudophenomenon, he suggests a "magnetic influence." The patterns of syntax, dictating the end of the sentence through the conjunction *because,* provide a stronger and more plausible cause, one that Bloom avoids mentioning. The balance of the watch's *going* and Boylan's *coming* (a verb suggested by the sentence would certainly have ironic overtones) is strongly implied by the structure of the sentence to be a causal balance. Bloom's using *because* sets up, by the determining patterns of the entelechic sentence, a situation that seemingly must be the case; the word itself comes to be, as it were, the causal connection for what Bloom will not mention.

Causality and movement in time are the protagonists in the agon of history, that nightmare which haunts Stephen. For him, history represents "a tale too often heard," one whose end, hardly discernible, often erratic, is probably malicious (these an Irishman's not unfounded suspicions). Speaking to the school director, Stephen gets another dose of history from the conqueror, an Orangeman: "All history moves towards one great goal, the manifestation of God" (34). Deasy's view is loosely derived from Hegel,[21] an unsubtle and Edwardian misunderstanding of the manifestation of the Universal Spirit. (Hegel says, "The final aim [of history] is God's purpose with the world.")[22] Stephen reacts strongly to the consequences of this view of history as a determined pattern, an irrevocable sequence of preordained events. It is indeed a nightmare from which one should try to awake. As Deasy articulates it, only historical necessity motivates individual acts; and Stephen is threatened by an historical determinism, a black panther that disturbs individual creativity.

Stephen had earlier toyed with and rejected Deasy's notion of historical determinism in the question that prompted his Aristotelian definition of the "actuality of the possible as possible": "Had Pyrrhus not fallen by a beldam's hand in Argos or Julius Caesar not been knifed to death? They are not to be thought away. Time has branded them and fettered they are lodged in the room of the infinite possibilities they have ousted. But can those have been possible seeing that they never were? Or was that only possible which came to pass? Weave, weaver of the wind" (25). Stephen tries to consider the idea that if some event were destined to happen, as necessary for the progress of history, then there could be no other possible event, and thus *possible* would only be a term one applied ex post facto (which is to use the term meaninglessly). The events of history are real, Pyrrhus was killed and Caesar was knifed; to think of things which were not actualized, not part of the unfolded process, is idle speculation, "weaving the wind." It is Stephen's predilection for Aristotle that makes him raise the question in this way, preparing for the answer supplied by entelechy, in this case the realization of an end inherent within something and not imposed upon it from without.

But the language of his own answer would have told Stephen as much as the definition by Aristotle. Its expressive form moves to actualize its own grammatical possibilities, symbolizing the movement of Pyrrhus and Caesar as they realize their historic potentialities in the arena of time: "Time has branded them and fettered they are lodged in the room of the infinite possibilities they have ousted." The *them* of the two great men at the start of the sentence is the object of time's action, *branded*. As the sentence proceeds, *them* turns to *they*. Caesar and Pyrrhus become subjects of the verb in the passive, *lodged;* but they are still being acted upon by time, being "fettered." The sentence moves through two prepositional phrases which maintain the movement by carrying through to their objects: *in* to *room* (the positional preposition is the note here of space within time), and *of* to *possibilities*. The sentence, moving rapidly without punctuation, comes to its end in an adjective clause which refers to the noun *possibilities*. In that clause the pronoun *they* reaches its final stage as well, as the subject of a transitive verb *oust*. Possibilities inherent at the beginning of the sentence within the grammatical parts—*them* as object, acted upon—are realized in the end—*they* as subject, acting. The historical process is paralleled by the syntactic one: men move from oppressed to oppressors as they move grammatically from object to subject. History and language march along in equal, entelechic steps.

Stephen rejects Deasy's view of history, and rightly, as the irrevocable progress of events without any individual character, events in a process dictated by something beyond and outside them. He rejects Deasy outright, if momentarily, by his contention that God is not the fixed end of history but the random cry of life in the street.[23] Nothing in Deasy's interpretation, in contrast to Aristotle, is integral to or inherent in the particular actors in time. Stephen needs to feel, as he has felt ever since the *Portrait*, the fullness of life's possibilities, the million encounters, all of which are matter awaiting the working hand of the artist to give them form. Life must present possibilities, and Stephen must be free to transform them, in order for the progress of his life to have any meaning, in order for him to become the artist within him, the creative prime mover.

What Stephen has done, in supplying an answer to the

Deasy view of history as necessity, is to order language in a particular way, giving it an integral sequence and a pattern which is not possible in a deterministic view. Stephen exercises the power of memory, that memory which keeps him integral in a world of changing molecules ("I . . . am I because my memory"), and in exercising it he engages in an activity of mind which organizes the facts and events of history, the reality of past experience. In a passage such as the one analyzed above, Stephen can be seen as being himself engaged in the artistic endeavor of which he spoke so proudly in the *Portrait:* his language forges art by the interaction of soul (here intelligence and memory) with the reality of (past historical) experience. It is this endeavor, of course, which Joyce carries on continally in the whole of *Ulysses*, but in that passage above Stephen seems to give weight to Mulligan's prediction that in ten years he could do the same.

Yet what Stephen sees lying implicitly in Deasy's view of history lies within the language of the novel as well; and the movement of language can enact a similar nightmare for certain characters. Joyce allows the consequences of syntactic entelechy to run to their limit in the context of the world of *Ulysses*. As with so much else, notably the order of language, Joyce emphasizes the less benign aspects of his syntax at the level of his characters. As the functional and mimetic order of syntax gives way to increasingly arbitrary patterns, so too the predictable growth within the sentences is transformed into determined direction. The inherent implications of predictability are stressed; Joyce makes the deterministic aspect of entelechy dominant in the context of the character's world, whereby the expressive form of language enacts for the characters the harsh facts of life, reality, and history. A seeming determinism creeps into the predictable syntactical patterns of its entelechic process. The impulse of the grammatical parts to their actualization is not affected by the stopping of the sentence, and, with the ordered syntax moving the phrases beyond their fragmented ends, the language moves on with a method of its own: it turns the possible and the causal into the necessary. In actualizing what lay within it as possible, it begins to complete the events it describes and so appears to bring those events by necessity into being.

Stephen can escape the apparently inexorable movement in language because he is in control of it. As has been noted before, his sentences are marked by his own order. For him (as for the artist-figure) entelechy of language is his creative freedom, he builds the progression into directed wholes: "a menace, a disarming, and a worsting" (21). The nouns move actively in participial form; yet the last noun brings the progression to an end with something of the finality of an absolute. The power of the artistic intelligence, exercised by means of ordering and patterning, rises above the flux of history, or the stress of the reality of experience, to make art. Stephen's sentences are moved, but he is the mover.

Poor Bloom, however, is the prime moved; too accomodating, too pliable, he appears as the target and the scapegoat of all of language's suggested determined tyranny. Bloom's thoughts are often centered on the effects of time and spoken in a language which works a temporal effect. A glance at a passage from "Nausicaa" shows the extent to which the expressive form of syntax in the guise of a temporally determined entelechy appears in Bloom's thinking.

> All quiet on Howth now. The distant hills seem.
> Where we. The rhododendrons. I am a fool perhaps.
> He gets the plums and I the plumstones. Where I
> come in. All that old hill has seen. Names change:
> that's all. Lovers: yum yum.
> Tired I feel now. Will I get up? O wait. Drained all
> the manhood out of me, little wretch. She kissed me.
> My youth. Never again. Only once it comes. Or hers.
> Take the train there tomorrow. No. Returning not the
> same. Like kids your second visit to a house. The new
> I want. Nothing new under the sun. Care of P. O.
> Dolphin's barn. Are you not happy in your? Naughty
> darling. At Dolphin's barn charades in Luke Doyle's
> house. Mat Dillon and his bevy of daughters: Tiny,
> Atty, Floey, Mamy, Louy, Hetty. Molly too. Eighty-
> seven that was. Year before we. And the old major
> partial to his drop of spirits. Curious she an only child,
> I an only child. So it returns. Think you're escaping
> and run into yourself. Longest way round is the short-
> est way home. And just when he and she. (377)

Bloom recognizes that 'history repeats itself,' a view only slightly less malevolent than Deasy's determinism, and from the beach at Sandymount sees the site of his love's consummation, Howth Head. "Where we" is his response to the memory; he will not say further, keeping time (the past) restricted to a certain place. Language, however, places him painfully where he is absent in his marriage: "He gets the plums and I the plumstones. Where I come in." Later on, thinking of another place (Dolphin's Barn) and the charades at Luke Doyle's where he first met Molly, he can no longer avoid time: "Year before we." Again he is caught up in linguistic order which suggests that time has tracks as unchangeable as life itself—"Longest way round is the shortest way home." As in Stephen's description of entelechy, it is to ourselves that we return.

Since he is unable to reconcile completely the flux of events with language, an unfinished sentence seems to take him where he does not wish to go. As so often during the day, he thinks about Boylan and Molly while on the beach in the evening: "And just when he and she" (377). Bloom's shame may prevent him from finishing this sentence, but a determined language knows no shame. The requirements of a temporary subordination indicate the time of the lovers' meeting, and the verb, specified as being the plural, is the volatile combination of *he* and *she*. What Bloom cannot bring himself to say about the harsh fact of Molly's adultery the syntax articulates for him, and with an apparent relentless determinism it presents the realization to him. Blazes and Molly are joined both verbally and venereally. The language's process, so much like that of life, makes the two movements equal and causally related: what the grammar fulfills in this sentence is the actualization of what occurs at 7 Eccles St. at 4:00 o'clock. To the confines of the physical world, expressed by the mechanical patterns of language, is here added the tyranny of the causal realm. Bloom is caught between the pincers of the physical and metaphysical worlds. The way he uses language only seems to thrust up against him, create for him, the very facts he is trying to forget.

There are other moments where language similarly takes Bloom too far. Often early and late in the day, Bloom tries not to think and not to speak about the impending adultery, as if somehow sensing that speaking, using the language, causes the adultery, indeed actualizes it: "Today.

Today. Not think" (180); "Think no more about that" (154). For Bloom, the passage of time only brings about the undesired end of his being cuckolded: "At four, she said. Time ever passing. Clockhands turning. On" (260). The passage of time is inevitable, the motion of sentences irrevocable, and the consequent adultery seems to be so too; he cannot avert it: "Stop. Stop. If it was it was. Must" (167). The imperative *must* states a strong case. Bloom even tries to speak away the time, as if by annihilating it he removes the impending adultery: "Then about six o'clock I can. Six, six. Time will be gone then. She . . ." (174). Once more the patterns of an entelechic language bring up the fact that he is trying to avoid, here in the form of an action, a verb. Like Stephen's historical possibilities, the cruel facts of Molly's unfaithfulness cannot be thought away, and the determined syntax reflects the harsh reality in seeming to force those facts on Bloom.

Joyce has thus allowed the order of language in its syntactic patterns to play out to its limit at the level of the characters in the universe of *Ulysses*. The language of order can and does enact the systems and activities of physical life with functional, mimetic realism; and, developing an entelechy of its own, it progresses into a temporal dimension as well. The patterns often stress mechanical aspects because they reflect the limits of the life they portray; they enact the mechanical in nature and demonstrate the limits of the physical. In their entelechy they can reflect the determination of life and the irrevocability of its harsh facts. Bloom is badly treated by life: he loses his only son, and his wife betrays him. Language's harsh patterns reflect that tyranny and apparent capriciousness.

Yet the artistic limits of language's order are pronounced in all its forms, even as Joyce indulges in them. While entelechy offers Joyce the means of displaying his involvement in his art by engaging a process in which he is the prime mover, and offers as well the manner for his language to pass from a spatial linearity to a suggested temporality, it also too strongly binds him to the order of syntax. As he takes the control of language right up to the end of its consequences, Joyce demonstrates the limited significance of all patterns and orders. Order and form are necessary to give meaning and proportion, and language of course relies on patterns; yet ultimately all orders are in some measure tyrannies not only for the characters in the novel but also for the artist in his art.

The patterns of language ultimately confine even at the level of the artist. Stephen sees the determinism of Deasy's view of history as a threat to individual creativity; similarly the generality and predictability of language's patterns, the determination of their own syntactic order, represent a challenge, if not an outright threat, to the individual creativity of the artist. While the system and patterns of language can be put to use by the artistic intellect to achieve much (even to recreate life), ultimately the sameness and universal nature of those systematic patterns hamper creativity, providing it only with limited means by which to exercise its artistic individuality. To follow the order of writing each chapter in a different mood, each with reference to an organ of the body, is no less an imposition than living as a character in a universe where life's patterns and those of language restrict and inhibit freedom.

Pound, writing on Joyce, claimed that "the artist cannot

afford to be ignorant of his limitations."[24] Joyce was aware of the inherent limitations of his own appropriate order, as the various excess patterns, both physical and metaphysical, show. He also makes his characters aware. Listening to the seductive music in "Sirens," music which is highly emotional and yet tightly patterned form, Bloom remarks: "Numbers it is. All music when you come to think. Two multiplied by two divided by half is twice one. . . . Do anything you like with figures juggling. Always find out this equal to that. . . . Musemathematics. And you think you're listening to the ethereal. But suppose you said it like: Martha, seven times nine minus x is thirty-five thousand. Fall quite flat" (278). The many examples in the last two chapters have come from sections of the novel which involve highly technical forms: musical ("Sirens"); corporeal ("Lestrygonians"); spatial ("Wandering Rocks"). Bloom himself senses that an excess of pattern, the presentation of the pattern at its most evident, is insufficient. "Words? Music? No: it's what's behind" (274).

What is behind is something whose expressive form is found in language open and free, suggestive and various. Joyce's syntax allows him not only order but also the license to transgress the limits of order, to pass to something else, more appropriate as a register of meaning for the other parts of his dialectic. It provides the characters a means to articulate their spirit and the artist an opportunity for unique creativity.

If we study the grammar, say, of the words "wishing," "think-ing," "understanding," "meaning," we shall not be dissatisfied when we have described various cases of wishing, thinking, etc. If someone said, "surely this is not all that one calls 'wishing,'" we should answer, "certainly not, but you can build up more complicated cases if you like." And after all, there is not one definite class of features which characterize all cases of wishing (at least not as the word is commonly used). If on the other hand you wish to give a definition of wishing, i.e., to draw a sharp boundary, then you are free to draw it as you like; and this boundary will never entirely coincide with the actual usage, as this usage has no sharp boundary.

Wittgenstein, *The Blue Book*

5 Appropriate Freedom and Variety

Joyce remarked in a conversation with Arthur Power about the "phenomena of modern life" that "when we are living a normal life we are . . . following a pattern which has been laid out by other people in another generation. . . . The eternal qualities are the imagination and the sexual instinct, and the formal life tries to suppress both."[1] This attitude is clearly anticlerical and very much the view of the late nineteenth century artist, yet there lies behind it a sense of some uneasiness other than that aimed at church or state. By extension there is a suspicion of all formal orders, not only society's conventions or a nation's laws, but, more to the point here, there is a distrust of the formal orders of language.

While order is a desideratum for a systematic mind like Joyce's—much can be accomplished by order and nothing

without it—there is something in Joyce's rebellious creativity that also makes him reject order; he is neither living
nor writing "normally." The order that lies at the heart
of language can, if too closely followed, lead to an almost
predictable, calculable series of expressions, creations, and
products. Amid the precision of grammar and the rules of
syntax there is a power of a system of universals which
holds sway over its material; all expressions and cases
are subsumed under dictated patterns, and much is suppressed. Most pointedly, order militates against the possibilities of plurality, ambiguity, and paradox which are also
so dear to Joyce and which are fertile fields of the imagination and instinct that order seeks to suppress.

Universal description, if not universal darkness, covers
all in *Ulysses*. Bloom the character is literally inundated
in this following passage from "Ithaca"; despite the several terms which denote him, he sinks beneath the surface
of the words and their tightened syntactic order:

> What in water did Bloom, waterlover, drawer of
> water, watercarrier returning to the range, admire?
> Its universality: its democratic equality and con-
> stancy to its nature in seeking its own level: its vastness
> in the ocean of Mercator's projection: its unplumbed
> profundity in the Sundam trench of the Pacific ex-
> ceeding 8,000 fathoms: the restlessness of its waves
> and surface particles visiting in turn all points of its
> seaboard. (671)

The general case, suggesting the predictable patterns both
in life and language, operates so as to diminish the very
things described.

Wittgenstein, in a moment of reflection, criticized the
universal view of philosophy. He accused his own field of a

"contemptuous attitude towards the particular case,"[2] of trying always to find the general and losing sight of what was unique. The encyclopedic form of *Ulysses* as a novel—indeed the encyclopedic and anatomic impulse in all fiction—is guilty of this same sin, of trying to assimilate the particular under a universal heading. The diminution of Bloom in stature and emphasis, as in the quotation above, is a direct result of the novel's encyclopedic tendency. There is a seeming contempt for the uniqueness of the characters in the late sections of the book as a variety of orders and structures comes into use.[3]

Joyce certainly valued order but he could not follow it as closely as he did without being able to deviate from it, without being able to say that he would not serve it. Rather than follow slavishly the order of language which could restrict his work and his world of the novel, he could exploit the appropriateness of his own order so that it would hamper less his creativity and confine less his characters' movement. A syntax even partially freed from regulation and pattern is an expressive form that permits particular rather than predictable constructions, a form that preserves individual expressions, making them unique precisely because they do not partake of order and pattern.

"The bungholes sprang open and a huge dull flood leaked out, flowing together, winding through mudflats all over the level land, a lazy pooling swirl of liquor bearing along wideleaved flowers of its froth" (79). There is, of course, much order to this sentence, notably alliterative morphemic patterns (a*ll* over *l*evel *l*and: *sw*irl of *l*iquor: *wide*leaved *fl*owers of *fr*oth); there is also the order of the two actions paralleled by verbs in the past tense, *sprang* and *leaked*. There follow two adjective clauses, a common feature of Joyce's style, again parallel in present participles, *flowing* and *winding*—whose antecedent, however, is less than clear (if "flood," why flowing "together"?). The last, a noun phrase, is absolute. Its composition also includes two participles, *pooling* and *bearing*, whose antecedent is the noun *swirl;* there is no verb, as the phrase does not complete a pattern. While beginning with a definite syntactic order, the sentence seems to float away grammatically, ending in a phrase which may echo the order of what preceded it but only does so to indicate its independent status.

Such independence is often achieved by simple means, by the sentence as non-sentence: "Near the timberyard a squatted child at marbles, alone, shooting the taw with a cunnythumb" (77) (note the inverted subject and predicate which changes verb to adjective); "Perched on high stools by the bar, hats shoved back, at the tables calling for more bread no charge, swilling, wolfing gobfuls of sloppy food, their eyes bulging, wiping wetted moustaches" (169); "North wall and sir John Rogerson's quay, with hulls and anchorchains, sailing westward, sailed by a skiff, a crumpled throwaway, rocked on the ferry-wash, Elijah is coming" (240) (the phrase "sailed by a skiff" might contain a declined verb, although both "sailing westward" and "rocked on the ferry-wash" as adjective phrases suggest otherwise). Those examples come from the narrative voice; this phrase from the monologue is independent in a more complicated way: "Healthy perhaps absorbs all the" (376). The sentences which seem to develop with their own entelechy are frequently interrupted in their syntax before a necessary verb or subordinating conjunction which would be tied to the grammatical system; in this sentence, however, what is missing is a noun, a unit which cannot be further defined by the syntax. It is this opening up of syntax that allows Joyce the means to transgress the boundaries of established order and system to create new possibilities of meaning.

Such possibilities and independence provide a means to protect the characters from assimilation into that order which makes them general and predictable, a way to avoid language which cannot express particulars. The characters must remain visible and noticeable among the increasing generalization in their novelistic world of patterns—physical, social, and linguistic. In an order appropriate in its loosened syntax, the characters can resist the patterns of language as well as the limited physical world those patterns represent. Silence was Dedalus's answer, a silence rich with artistic meaning. As a burgeoning artist he often comes to use language and not be used by it; he anticipates the processes of language by becoming their originator, their prime mover, and thus he occasionally puts them at his control. Art, however, is not a vocation to which everyone is called, and Bloom is the prime moved. A reluctance to speak, through this silence denying the necessary and inevitable patterning in language which represents a corresponding inevitability in life, is a first response for a character like Bloom.

When Bloom writes to Martha Clifford while at the Ormond Bar, he needs to be circumspect lest Goulding, sitting opposite him, catch on; consequently his thought is interrupted by caution. "Accept my poor little pres enclos. . . . Write me a long. Do you despise? Jingle, have you the?" (279). The first three sentences are parts of actual sentences Bloom puts on paper while guarding his writing; the last, however, is a sentence interrupted for reasons other than caution. The phrase is Bloom's repetition of Lenehan's comment to Boylan, as the latter impatiently leaves the bar at 4:00; the word left off is *horn*, the mark of the cuckold. It becomes, like the word *cuckold* itself, a word of fear; Bloom's refusal to think it is an attempt to avoid selfrecrimination. Thus broken sentences, in independent unrelated parts, try to end the progress of language which the character sees looming before him. Here is Bloom, so often symbolically the victim of determined progression, early in the day at the newspaper office: "I could go home still: tram: something I forgot. Just to see before dressing. No. Here. No" (123). He thinks of the possibility of returning to glimpse Molly before Boylan arrives; he thinks of a way to travel and even an excuse. There seem to be time ("still") and means of motion ("tram"); the lovers' difficulties of "world enough and time" might be surmountable. Yet the possibility here would only result in embarassment. The sentences which would move him to that familiar end are broken off in their potential progress by a terse finality: "No. Here. No." Bloom's denial insists on the present place and time without any condition, insists on them curtly, and refuses to encourage the progress of language which will only develop later into pain. He would be embarrassed not only by the probable situation, but also by the realization of a syntactic one: if the sentences were allowed to carry to their ends, they would present a case he wishes to avoid like the actual event.

116

This negation, breaking off sentences firmly before they develop their consequences, is Bloom's frequent reflex.

> Some chap with a dose burning him.
>   If he . . .
>   O!
>   Eh?
>   No . . . No.
>   No, no. I don't believe it. He wouldn't surely?
>   No, no.
>   Mr Bloom moved forward raising his troubled eyes.
> Think no more about that. (153–54)

The tentative syntactic constructions "if he" and "he wouldn't surely," constructions whose ends are well known to Bloom, are stopped by emphatic denial. Six negatives divert the potential progress which would trouble Bloom. He even gives himself a command to stop both his thinking and its articulation in the leading syntax. Later in the same chapter he repeats the truncating command: "Not think" (180). To the resounding "yes" of Molly's affirmation of life, Bloom, caught in the parallel toils both of that life and of language, sends out a qualified "no."

Improbable as it may at first appear, a form of silence, a reticence of expression, seems therefore to be at work throughout the world of the book. In order to avoid the general thrust of the excessive patterning of language and the apparently inevitable consequences inherent in it, what is important, deep, and emotional for the characters ought to be said by them in a few words. Something must be able to be expressed in terms other than those of language's order. At the level of the characters, the book actually posits a sort of inverse ratio, wherein what is least important is expressed in the greatest number of words, and what is most important in the fewest. Beleaguered Bloom's poignant and short "I'm talking about injustice" in the argument in "Cyclops" becomes lost in the mass of words which the citizen utters in his false patriotism and which the narrator then carries formally to the limits of comic inflation. The long and cliché-ridden passages in "Eumaeus" mask Bloom's very curt and thus earnest concern for Stephen. Penny-novel romance covers over with its too-heavy rhetorical perfume the insubstantiality of Gerty's love for Reggie Wylie, and it also serves as a screen for her deformity. In so far as parody and pastiche are the exploitation of form at the expense of substance, the use of various styles in "Oxen" to record the more monotonous than monumental birth of yet another Purefoy may again demonstrate this ratio. Indeed in the second half of the book where the chapters increase in length, this ratio appears most frequently; there is a talking all round the important emotions, never approaching them by reason of sheer verbal excess and pattern. "Ithaca," with its universal detail, excessively patterned and limited as it is, certainly is a prime example.

In "Circe" amid Bella-Bello's various diatribes against Bloom and his sexual activity, Bloom speaks out several disconnected words: "Forgive. Moll! . . . we . . . Still . . ." (541). In their independence from syntax and their poignant brevity these few words are a source of deep emotion—perhaps even a promise for Bloom's marriage on and after June 17, perhaps only a wish, but something far weightier than the few words themselves.

Language with highly evident patterns and elaborate

design in some sense is a structural facade, like the Enlightenment architectural facades of Dublin buildings which belie the unenlightened life beneath and behind. The mechanical forms possible within language's system, while they can be expressive, also can be a heavy order under which more fragile things must labor; they cast things in a certain form. The following exchange in the *Portrait* of Stephen with the priest on the aesthetics of words is illuminating in this regard: "The language in which we are speaking is his before it is mine. How different are the words *home, Christ, ale, master,* on his lips and on mine! I cannot speak or write these words without unrest of spirit. His language, so familiar and so foreign, will always be for me an acquired speech. I have not made or accepted its words. My voice holds them at bay. My soul frets in the shadow of his language" (189). This is not only a patriotic problem for Stephen; he would, after all, not die for his country. Rather he uses a patriotic rhetoric, again as facade, to express a concurrent, but for him deeper, linguistic and aesthetic problem.

In *Ulysses,* Stephen thinks of the three nets that have trapped him: "Three nooses round me here. Well. I can break them" (30). The snare of history and that of family he can meet, but that of language is the gordian knot that is hardest to cut. Stephen feels this entrapment several times during the day. As he listens to Mr. Deasy's sententious morality and history, he sees in the old man the representation of the empire and remembers Haines earlier in the morning: "The seas' ruler. His seacold eyes looked on the empty bay: history is to blame: on me and on my words, unhating" (30). Both Stephen and the art he is trying to create are controlled through patterns (here represented by the order of the sentence and the prepositions: "on me and on my words").

Similarly the pull of his family, a death-hold on him, is strengthened through language. He thinks of his mother: "Her glazing eyes, staring out of death, to shake and bend my soul. On me alone" (10). Patterns of language bind Stephen; much like the almost tyrannical entelechy of Bloom's sentences, they relate him to the things he is trying to escape. Stephen fears that his mother's ghost will strike him down, and his soul cries out against it: "No Mother, let me be and let me live. . . . Stephen, still trembling at his soul's cry" (107). What that apparition tries to do is to force conventionality on him, in the guise of the accepted forms of church worship. These are conventions which Stephen (as well as Joyce, as he said to Power) always must reject. Similarly (and by a chain of association) language tries to shake Stephen's spirit by making it assume accepted forms, be it Mulligan's verbal taunts or Deasy's linguistic imperialism. Stephen must use language cautiously, his own words and not others' dictated ones. Weak and undervalued, his spirit fits uneasily with these forms and waits like Ariel for the magic stroke of art to free it from its cloven pine.

True to the paradoxical in him, Joyce the wordsmith, the conscious craftsman, was often uneasy with his own words. Even while being lionized in Paris, he deliberately covered his many years of painful creativity with such off-handed comments as this to Djuna Barnes: "There is not one single serious line" in *Ulysses*.[4] In his courtship of Nora, Joyce could plead, "Can you not see the simplicity which is at the back of all my disguises?"[5] A contemporary of his youth commented, "The gestures he made with the ashplant . . . , his way of making his voice raucous, were surely part of an act."[6] His distant soul may after all have been simple and sentimental; Stanislaus says he "wept when he sang 'The Bells of Shandon.' "[7] There were moments when Joyce felt himself to be a poseur, taking a stance against the world in the ways of the world; and the disguises were both physical and verbal. The tension in Joyce's creativity may be viewed as being between impersonal pattern and deep emotion, and the language gave him the means to accommodate both.[8] The stance of the aloof artist-god was a pose too, one which masked the intense concern Joyce had for the smallest part of his creation and which covered the sentimental with a veneer. Constantly in his career there was the awareness that his art of language must by necessity take form and pattern, but that in so doing it screened emotions and imagination, the provinces respectively of character and author-figure.

Stephen, as fledgling artist, seems to share the unease of his creator when he asks, "Who ever anywhere will read these written words?" (48). He too is a poseur: "My Latin Quarter hat. God, we must simply dress the character. I want puce gloves" (41). Stephen often uses the forms of language to cover up his emotions: his phrase "Agenbite of Inwit," which recurs through the novel, is an archaic and literary term, used as a sign to mark a host of very painful memories and emotions.[9] Stephen is himself aware that he uses his learning and language as a screen to cover his spirit. Debating whether he would save a man from drowning as Mulligan did, Stephen considers: "But the courtiers who mocked Guido in Or san Michele were in their own house. House of . . . We don't want any of your medieval abstrusiosities." He keeps himself from avoiding the question by repeating, "Would you do what he did? . . . Would you or would you not?" Finally, he must tell himself sternly: "The truth, spit it out. I would want to. I would try. I am not a strong swimmer" (45). The answer, following the hypothetical inverse ratio, is distinct, uncomplicated, and poignantly direct: "I would try." A little later he says, thinking of his mother, "I could not save." The soft core of Stephen, the weak soul hidden underneath the Latin Quarter hat, is armoured over with the steel of art and with the abstrusiosities and graces of an often too finely patterned and polished language.

Faced with the very painful fact of his mother's death and the force of convention her death wish represents, Stephen uses his language both as a shield and a veil. Mulligan, defending his statement that Stephen's mother was beastly dead, "had spoken himself into boldness."

> Stephen, shielding the gaping wounds which the words had left in his heart, said very coldly:
> —I am not thinking of the offence to my mother.
> —Of what then? Buck Mulligan asked.
> —Of the offence to me, Stephen answered. (8-9)

Language here is a pose and a defense. Stephen changes the objects of the prepositions ("to my mother," "to me") to deflect the thrust of language; and the wounded heart and weak spirit are protected. Appearing early in the novel, this passage shows again clearly that behind the patterns there is a spirit and heart uneasily covered by the forms language must take.

Stephen's covering over the tender with the abstruse and Bloom's terse, reluctant prevention of the inevitable are two parallel strategies to keep what is essential and integral to them from the universality of the patterned language and the general case. Not to say what is most true and dear is to keep it inviolate, to hold it aloof from the crowd, like the boy in the story "Araby" who carries the chalice amid the host of foes. Terseness retains some part of the self; and it should come as no surprise that pronouns figure prominently in this strategy. Whereas at times the pronouns appear to reinforce the patterning and system of language, at others the pronouns appear independently as if to symbolize the retention of part of the self.

Even the egotistical Stephen, mastering language, cannot avoid feeling vulnerable to the slings and arrows of the linguistic world around him and must preserve his identity in this way. Moments after he forces himself to confront the fact of his own cowardice in being unable to save a drowning man, he thinks how Mulligan may be displeased with him: "He now will leave me. And the blame? As I am. As I am" (49). Whatever Mulligan will do (and note how Stephen contorts both language and fact to say that Mulligan will leave him), Stephen remains firm; he stays true to his stubborn and self-pitying decision, but also true to what he is and must be as a person. He expresses his individuality in terms as absolute as the God of Sinai; the repetition of the first person pronoun asserts the self unequivocally, without predication, as pure being.

Faced with the difficulties of penury and little poetry, Stephen comes close to despair: "The whirr of flapping leathern bands and hum of dynamos from the powerhouse urged Stephen to be on. Beingless beings. Stop! Throb always without you and the throb always within. Your heart you sing of. I between them. Where? Between two roaring worlds where they swirl, I" (242). He sees himself existing between machines, the external, impersonal dynamos of the powerhouse and the internal workings of his own body, and he notes that his self, the "I," stands independently between the inner and outer systems, even as it stands independently in the syntax of the last sentence. He recognizes as well that the self needs the machinery of its own being: it could not exist without the necessary functions of its system. Yet, in despair, Stephen considers capitulating to the order that exists all around him; he ponders the result of such striking out against machinery: "Shatter them, one and both. But stun myself in the blow. Shatter me you who can. . . . Not yet awhile." He abandons what seems to be an idea of suicide; he will make more time to sing songs of the heart. The self can be made strong through art and a freer, unconventional language to triumph over the power of all forms of machinery, internal and external; order can be appropriated. At other points in the day Stephen's uneasiness with his own being is clearly and succinctly expressed. He is aware of his isolation, and his words stress the reciprocal balance of his solitude: "I spoke to no-one; none to me" (45).

Existence in *Ulysses* is by no means an obvious thing. Thanks to coincidence there are, after all, two Leopold Blooms. The general trend to assimilate all particulars under a general rule is a threat to the characters which is perhaps more real than Bloom's fear of a suicide caused by the "aberration of the light of reason." In this large book of schemes and plans, formal and verbal, there are many questions of existence. The puzzle of Mr. W. H., to whom Shakespeare dedicated his sonnets, occupies all the pundits in the library, and Stephen's question "W. H.: who am

I?" (198) is not easily answered. It remains one of the un-
solved problems in the literary world, faintly limning the
elusive shadow of self represented by the single pronoun *I*.

Language, as a pattern and universal order, symbolizes
this pervasive threat to existence. The problematic M'Intosh, it should be remembered, owes his naming to a misunderstanding in language:

> —And tell us, Hynes said, do you know that fellow
> in the, fellow was over there in the . . .
> He looked around.
> —MacIntosh. Yes, I saw him, Mr Bloom said. Where
> is he now?
> —M'Intosh, Hynes said, scribbling, I don't know
> who he is. Is that his name? (112)

M'Intosh thus is baptized merely by the coat he is wearing,
the language like the raincoat cloaking the mystery underneath.

M'Intosh also serves to represent the unknowable opposite with whom one barely comes in contact. For all the
relations between members of society, it is seen how frail
unions are, how alone Bloom remains. He is an outsider,
and himself a puzzle to those around him.[10] Nosey Flynn's
contention that Bloom is in the craft only adds to rather
than detracts from the mystery. Posing a similar question,
Bloom asks of children, "What do they love?" (379); and
the answer he gives himself, "another themselves," seemingly ungrammatical, encompasses within a pronoun the
puzzle of both the individual and the other. Bloom tries to
escape fate by a change in pronoun—"he, not me" (381)—
while Stephen, afraid of being arrested in Paris for murder,
claims the existence of an "other me" (41). Stephen also
daydreams about women, a legacy from the *Portrait* days

of E. C. and Mercedes: "She trusts me, her hand gentle, the longlashed eyes." Yet this figure is only an ideal, and he crossly asks himself if there is any identity behind the fantasy: "She, she, she. What she?" (48). Molly's ease in substituting the masculine pronoun for any individual similarly suggests puzzles of identity. Her list of lovers, that source of much controversy, while having the aura of specificity is no more clear than her statement "I thought as well him as another."

Bloom is always acutely aware of himself. He is often uneasy in company—"Glad I took that bath" (89)—and knows when others make fun of him (for example, the newsboys). He is careful to speak in such a way as to keep his self, through the references to himself, from being caught up in all the patterns of language whose consequences are painfully beyond him. At Davy Byrne's he thinks lyrically of his courtship of Molly on Howth, his former success and joy; he thinks abruptly, "Me. And me now" (176). Again the pronoun asserts itself. While not in the nominative, rather declined, it is not evident where this could be placed grammatically. It is very unlike the nighttown watch's accusatory "Bloom. Of Bloom. For Bloom. Bloom" (453); it is more like an independent statement of the fact of Bloom's existence. The short phrase brings up the change in him from the memory of success to the current cuckoldry, but it does so in ways that forestall the process and the patterned side of language which are represented by the reciprocal "Kissed, she kissed me." The phrase takes a large quantum leap in time, springing over all the sequence of events that have led up to the current set of circumstances; and it insists on the central point, the *me,* the individual and not the system. There is the adultery; it is always present in the world going on around Bloom, and is something he has not started and can hardly prevent. Yet in its midst, in the march of life and language's seemingly irrevocable pace, he salvages and sustains part of himself.

In a similar manner, after his erotic but empty encounter with Gerty, Bloom tries to leave a message in the sand.

> Mr Bloom with his stick gently vexed the thick sand at his foot. Write a message for her. Might remain. What?
> I. . . .
> AM. A. (381)

All in capitals, the last cry of an isolated man, it proclaims his existence, if only that, in the face of a hostile world and in the surface of the futile sand. Like Stephen's "as I am," it is Bloom's absolute assertion of self. In his notesheets for this episode, Joyce wrote to himself, "B. writes in sand, what?"[11] Both he and Bloom found an answer which was not an answer but rather the opening of a greater mystery.

This faded message—it is even erased by Bloom himself —proclaims Bloom in big letters, and does so because it asserts itself in a very particular way. One asks in wonder what the completion of this could be. Unlike the sentences of inherently determined possibilities, this has no preordained pattern. The completion could be either an adjective (alone), an article and noun (a man), or some other predicate adjective or predicate nominative. Nothing can be decided definitely. Rather than belong to a predictable syntactic development, this sentence seems to jump out of the tracks of language's patterns. It is left off by Bloom

and Joyce at precisely a most important moment. Here is a
gap in the system of language, an area where the unknown
reigns with any multitude of possibilities, not predeter-
mined ones. Everything can be predicated on mere existence. Rather than resisting the patterns of language with
posture and evasion, a character who avoids the structures
gets free by jumping beyond to levels of variety where
limits end and boundaries lose their edge. Not expressed
in patterns, one can be free. Bloom responds similarly in
thinking about Martha Clifford, the mystery lover known
to him only through her ill-spelt letters: "She's a" (275).
He is not sure what she is, only that she is someone particular.[12] When he suspects one of the Ormond Bar maids
as being his secret correspondent, he is reluctant to name:
"Suppose she were the?" (286). Even the flower Martha
sends him by mail is left uncatalogued: "A flower. I think
it's a" (77). One of the forty respondents to his inquiry,
Martha is special for his having chosen her and so cannot
be included in a general category.

What Joyce has done with this use of language is to exploit the area at the other end of his language's appropriate
order so as to revitalize its creative powers. The meaning
of words or the grammar of words is consequently open to
all sorts of possibilities; these holes in the order of language are appropriate to his purposes because they make
the unstated independent of system, unique in being not
dictated by rules. The semantic value of words unwritten
or disordered is rich with ambiguity and potential paradig-
matic depth. Each unstated word, freed from a syntactic
order that would seek to delineate it, has an integrity of its
own and a value commensurate with its independence. It
is a unique linguistic utterance, a single syntactic occur-

rence; and while a host of possibilities might suggest themselves as the correct one, it is in the richness of possible words, and not the opposite determination of a single word, that the unique quality of language lies. A sentence such as "the air feeds most" (71) displays just this variety of language. *Most* is either the qualifier of an adverb or an adjective; the various possible words, each with a valid, if pluralistic, claim in the syntax of the sentence, attest to the power of language's uniqueness.

When Stephen jocularly suggests the programme of a French bordelle to Bella and her associates, his imitation of English as spoken by a Frenchman instantly reduces normal syntax, and the effect is a confusion of phrases and single words: "Enter gentlemen to see in mirrors every positions trapezes all that machine there besides also if desire act awfully bestial butcher's boy pollutes in warm veal liver or omelette on the belly *pièce de Shakespeare*" (570). Both "trapeze" and "that machine there" are given an independent status by the absence of syntax in this sentence, as if by way of enhancing their erotic mystery.

Bloom's thoughts while dozing on the strand after his fireworks are conveyed in a language whose syntax has ceded place to the immediacy of the words themselves: "O sweety all your little girlwhite up I saw dirty bracegirdle made me do love sticky we two naughty Grace darling she him half past the bed met him pike hoses frillies for Raoul to perfume your wife black hair heave under embon *señorita* young eyes Mulvey plump years dreams return tail end Agendath swoony lovey showed me her next year in drawers return next in her next her next" (382). The order of syntax struggles to assert itself—"up I saw," "made me do love sticky"—yet falls finally to the insistent rhythm of various individual words of great purport: "Showed me her next year in drawers return next in her next her next." There "next year in Jerusalem," Agendath, and the East blend at the emotional level with "years dreams return" and the eastern dream of Molly in turkish drawers; there are also Bloom's return home to 7 Eccles and perhaps other attempts at intimacy with Molly, other chances. All these associations are made by the words themselves, paradigmatically freed from the order that syntax seeks to impose.

The expressive form of Joyce's language is used here to this particular end: the uniqueness of each character is maintained by the appropriateness of language unique and undetermined. Language does not necessarily separate characters from their dilemmas and needs; rather it can work to assert the validity of their feelings, if it does not necessarily describe them explicitly. The last two examples above concern the intimate thoughts of Stephen and Bloom: that their language is so opened as to be free of pattern is no accident.

The meaning of Joyce's appropriate order lies in a particular area. The parts of language which refuse to fit the patterns of syntax are precisely those incidents of the particular case where the individual triumphs over the universal and the general rule. Wittgenstein focused his attention on those structures which he said did not fit the calculus of language, because these structures interested him especially because of their difference.[13] They seemed to represent what in fact they did not; they appeared to be part of the calculus but defied it and expressed something else. Similarly, the uniqueness of Joyce's appropriate order expresses something else.

The order of language is highly denotative; syntax exerts a determining and exact effect on what will be. Words, phrases, and sentences are subordinated to the systematic patterning; all parts are positioned, fastened, and hence specifically denoted. A loosened syntax, however, precisely in not making things fixed and exact, in being open, is rich with possibilities and is potentially lyric. (One is reminded in this of I. A. Richards's division of language into the referential and the emotive. Within his own dual language, Joyce can have both modes for his characters and for himself.) The ordered side of language as system has predominantly philosophical implications; it is rational and deductive, general and universal. In addition, it enacts the processes of the physical world. What the opened order creates is unique, not fixed or subordinated into a general pattern. Inductive and even irrational, the free side allows for expression of the individual case and the emotions and imagination that are suppressed by order.

There are, of course, few occurrences where language tries directly to obliterate those patterns which give it meaning, or where it tries to use them as little as possible. The freedom of Joyce's order exists most significantly in contrast to that order itself: as noted earlier, the terms are by necessity relative. Yet there are examples enough to show that Joyce does represent this radical direction by means of an open syntax. Eating alone in Davy Byrne's moral pub, the normally abstemious Bloom drinks a glass of burgundy. The wine triggers in him a lyrical description:

> Glowing wine on his palate lingered swallowed. Crushing in the winepress grapes of Burgundy. Sun's heat it is. Seems to a secret touch telling me memory. Touched his sense moistened remembered. Hidden

under wild ferns on Howth. . . . O wonder! . . . Softly
she gave me in my mouth the seedcake warm and
chewed. Mawkish pulp her mouth had mumbled sweet
and sour with spittle. Joy: I ate it: joy. . . . She kissed
me. I was kissed. All yielding she tossed my hair.
Kissed, she kissed me.

Me. And me now. (175–76)

Parts of this passage have been encountered before: the
reciprocal balance in the language representing the alternating balance in emotional relationships ("Kissed, she
kissed me") or the reticent and protective "Me. And me
now." There is at this point no need to discuss the characteristic Joycean construction of participles used as adjective: "Touched his sense moistened remembered." Of
particular interest here is the phrase "Seems to a secret
touch telling me memory." There are no rules of grammar,
no orders of calculus in which this fits; the absence of even
a copula reduces the power. The wine's "touch" is both a
literal and metaphoric usage, and the touch's "telling" indicates a synaesthesia which further opens out the limits
of language. The entire phrase knows no bounds, it does
not rest in the realm of verifiable claims; it is rather the
expression of a particular moment of feeling which belongs to the individual uttering it and to no general
scale; it has a unique semantic value. Many meanings, and
none capturable by a pattern, lie in this: "Joy: I ate it:
joy." Many different grammatical parts, many possible
referents are applicable here, adverb or noun. All are un-
specified, and the more open and free for being so. The
freedom of language in these examples consists in the
leaps of feeling and faith which spring around the order of
language and the physical it represents. There can be no

bounds; wherever the line is drawn, as Wittgenstein says in the epigraph to this chapter, the particular usage goes beyond.

Stephen too speaks in this opened language. While playing the piano in the brothel, he comments to himself: "Play with your eyes shut. Imitate pa. Filling my belly with husks of swine. Too much of this. I will arise and go to my. Expect this is the" (517). He is trying to express his feelings and even his guilt about his father. His sentences are personal and are accordingly without their characteristic polished form. He alludes to the parable of the prodigal son and perhaps to Yeats's "Lake Isle of Innisfree." Yet his language is beyond parables, poems, and patterns. Nouns should come as referents for *my* and *the,* but there is no way to determine them. The language is open and so loose that there is no system that can be imposed upon it.

It is important to note that among the terms considered by Wittgenstein as being the most predominantly open and free are verbs dealing with emotions. Terms for emotions are without a doubt the most particular and least readily universalized in language. As Wittgenstein points out, this is owing to the fact that the constructions involving emotions are often intransitive, having no objects.[14] Thus they do not readily fall into the gaps in a calculus, the system of syntax. Wittgenstein's notion can be used to throw some light on the workings of Joyce's language. Direct objects, or active verbs, which are so readily solved in the ordered calculus and entelechy of language, are related to the parts around them by the requirements and the patterns of syntax. These solvable parts of a calculus may also be restricted in space and time and thus further recognizable. Moreover they recreate patterns which are observable in physical life. Emotions, on the other hand, are not bound by space and time—indeed are even suppressed by formal patterns. Not representable, they are timeless and free.

Bloom reflects on the poignant differences between himself and Boylan: "He gets the plums and I the plumstones" (377). The language is balanced, the syntax equitably parallel, and the patterns of nominalization seem to present the difference between plums and plumstones. Yet there is something here that cannot be produced through the linguistic patterns; it is the emotional difference between the two words. An entire novel's emotional weight, the force and feel of Bloom's loneliness, can only be treated by the patterns of language in a false equation. The emotional difference is vast, and the structures of language, here shown incapable in their order, cannot begin to bridge it. It is clear why sex can be treated in terms of mechanics, with necessary deflation and without too much detriment, because sex is merely a physical activity: the fixed principle best and most vividly enacts physical activity by means of its patterns. The emotional aspect of Bloom's cuckoldry, however, is not reducible to the patterned aspect of life or language; it is a separate dimension, one which needs and finds its own language in terms which are unbound and independent. The open and free functioning of Joyce's language is, at the level of the characters, that of the emotions of the human heart. The free constructions counterbalance and even undermine the planned and ordered language which enacts the physical.

Enthralled by the seductive charm of music, that emotional but highly patterned art, Bloom thinks about the language of love: "Tipping her tepping her tapping her topping her. Tup. Pores to dilate dilating. Tup. The joy the feel the warm the" (274). The first sentence has previously been cited as an example of patterns of language which reproduce physical ones; the second displays the usual play of verb and participle. The last, however, points to the other side of language. Made up of highly subjective words, listed independently without order or subordination, this phrase is one to which Bloom's own feelings lay claim. It does not recreate physical patterns nor suggest causal connections; the words just are there. In unordered language, this phrase is as incontrovertible as Bloom himself.

When Bloom asks himself about his former happiness— "Was that I? Or am I now I?" (168)—there can be no definite answer. Only Bloom himself can determine which relative state of happiness is greater: compare his "My joy is other joy" (282). There is no external standard, only what is privately intense and important to Bloom. More significantly, at the level of syntax the grammar cannot give a clue to further linguistic elaboration. The personal pronoun here stands free from patterns. What could follow "am I now I?" It is a basic question at the level of identity. The previous sentence in this example asks a parallel question of identity—something like "was that I in those times?"—but nothing is specified either by syntax or context. The pronoun is alone and hence untrammeled and free. It is indefinable but indisputable, like the expressions of existence noted before.

Therein, however, lies the infinite cold of insterstellar space and the puzzle of life's bitter mystery. The freedom bred by these jumps in language is one which brings as its price for Joyce's characters an unanswerable questioning of the open and infinite. In his notesheets to "Ithaca," that most studied of chapters, Joyce marked cryptically: "infinity = escape from hypothesis 0 proved ∞."[15] What he sought was a leap to something beyond order, endless and all-possible; he found the formula within his own language. The mechanical and entelechic sentences of order, in their marshalled patterns, give the sense that they complete themselves, even if fragmented. In their accountability and determination they seem to brook no questions, and they give the expectation of finality. Yet if the comfort of such completion can also be a limit, to leap to the freedom of language, to an emotional openness without pattern, is not without its dangers—the insecurity, mystery, and even wonder of a world made open to all semantic choices, to a variety of particular cases. There could be any number of answers to Bloom's questions; he cannot hope to answer them himself. Life is a mystery, and the language which most faithfully expresses that life must be a puzzle. There is no one word to say it all; there are many words which, patterned, delineate life exactly, and which, free, open up to it.

Stephen asks his mother's apparition in "Circe," "Tell me the word, mother, if you know. The word known to all men" (581). He asks the impossible of a shadow; it is a misleading question. The mystery of life and love admit of no one answer, one universal word for all. Each man has his many words, some unique and meaningful to him. It seems odd that Stephen should ask this question, which sounds more like Neoplatonism than his revered Aristotelianism. In a highly emotional moment, Stephen shows that he has, indeed, much to learn. Unable to accept the relative forms of language, he reaches toward an opposite extreme and

looks for an absolute. June 16 is for him clearly another of
many beginnings; he must wait the full decade until he
can write a *Ulysses.* Trying to escape the insistence of a
determined view of history, he correctly wants to assert
the fullness of life's possibilities; he even uses language to
create those possibilities: his sentences on Pyrrhus do what
history did not. In asking for the *word,* however, he in-
consistently wants a universal. Despite his gospel reading
and his Catholic education, his chosen career should tell
him that an artist needs *words,* many words; with them he
must seek out and talk to the mystery, and through the
words give it expression. Not to have his soul fret in language, he must use all of it, making each word appropriate
to his needs. Here is the gulf that ultimately separates
Joyce from the autobiographical figure, Stephen. Stephen
is not complete; rather it is the mature artist, Joyce, who
uses both order and appropriate order.

Bloom, indefatigable seeker after truth, makes a similar
mistake; he "himself had applied to the works of William
Shakespeare more than once for the solution of difficult
problems in imaginary or real life." His search is futile:

> Had he found their solution?
> In spite of careful and repeated reading of certain
> classical passages, aided by a glossary, he had derived
> imperfect conviction from the text, the answers not
> bearing on all points. (677)

Literary texts are not sacred scriptures (and this should be
a corrective to Joyce idolatry). Literature is not an answer,
or at least not all answers to all questions; it, like the life it
mirrors, leaves points unresolved. Even the rigid catechism of "Ithaca" is made up of answers which fail the

questions (as well as questions that fail the answers). The license of language only cultivates and represents that core of uncertainty which lies at the center of the universe of *Ulysses*.

Coincidence reigns in that world, and mechanical precision; and charts, maps, times, and organs give the novel the veneer of concrete reality. Yet behind all the schemes lies the mystery of life: the small mysteries of characters like M'Intosh; of plot (where did Bloom go between seeing Gerty and visiting Mina Purefoy?); of textual allusions to books and songs; and, most profoundly, of the emotions of love, friendship, and loyalty. What the order in language does for the mimetic precision of *Ulysses* at the surface level of reality in the novel, the free side does for its ambiguous mystery.[16] The novel prizes this equally with the order. Life is physical, and it is represented fully and graphically by the fixed principle; yet at the center of life lies a manifold mystery, and language must represent that as well. Sparse and suggestive, the free principle asks the fundamental but unanswerable questions about the characters' spirits and emotions by giving them expression.

The appropriateness of Joyce's order particularly expresses the characters' intellectual search for knowledge and understanding of the world in which they live. Questions from "Ithaca" mark the puzzle that Stephen and Bloom face about the inexplicable phenomena of repetitive physicality and determined progress which are their existence.

> Why did he [Bloom] desist from speculation?
> Because it was a task for a superior intelligence to substitute other more acceptable phenomena in place of the less acceptable phenomena to be removed.

138

> Did Stephen participate in his dejection?
> He affirmed his significance as a conscious rational
> animal proceeding syllogistically from the known to
> the unknown and a conscious rational reagent between
> a micro- and a macrocosm ineluctably constructed
> upon the incertitude of the void.
> Was this affirmation apprehended by Bloom?
> Not verbally. Substantially.
> What comforted his misapprehension?
> That as a competent keyless citizen he had pro-
> ceeded energetically from the unknown to the known
> through the incertitude of the void. (697)

Bloom's "void" is the black area of space through which
he falls in order to get to the entryway of his house; Stephen's is much more speculative. Yet both men, in their
particular ways, seek to respond intellectually to the void
of incomprehensible life through which they pass every
day. While that life, in its physical form, is vividly imitated
by the ordered principle of Joyce's language, the freer
principle attempts to express a feeling for and understanding of it. The mystery of the characters' existence, rendered by the appropriateness, is as real as the physical
enactments rendered by the order itself. By attempting to
face their mysteries and to search for the meaning of their
daily lives, through a language which speaks to the void,
the characters assert their validity as thinking and feeling
individuals; they employ a language so free as to be appre-
hended "not verbally. Substantially."

For Stephen and for Bloom—the diffident son and the
different father—questions of paternity ask again for the
solutions of life's and love's bitter mysteries. The surety of
Aristotle's biological process is here subjected to the presence of the ineffable that is also part of both life and

language. Paternity, which was a physical and artistic inevitability in one order of language, becomes in the dimensions of the other an essential question about the
nature of life. Telling his parable of the midwives to the
individuals en route to Mooney's pub, Stephen mentions
an address in Dublin that has particular meaning for him,
Fumbally's lane.

> —Where's that? the professor asked.
> —Off Blackpitts.
> Damp night reeking of hungry dough. Against the
> wall. Face glistening tallow under her fustian shawl.
> Frantic hearts. . . . Quicker, darlint!
> On now. Dare it. Let there be life. (145)

The essence of this furtive experience lies not in its un-
comfortable urgency but rather in its quality of physical
malleability: the synaesthetic (and thus incalculable)
"hungry dough," the "tallow." These are qualities which
approximate primal matter, existing to be made into something else; we can see how important Aristotle is for Stephen when he forms the memory in those terms: the
fustian shawl conveys just such a sense of coarse physical
quality. Stephen molds language here in a truly creative
(if Aristotelian) way, as he conflates the biblical with natural creation: "Let there be life." Yet the analogous processes of art and nature, seemingly fixed and determined,
are not absolute; the imperative voice is not enough to
bring forth life. A little later in the day, discussing Shakespeare and paternity, Stephen asks himself, "Am I father?
If I were?" (208). Enlightenment does not follow his act;
and only more uncertain questioning is the result of "fran-
tic hearts" and of free words which represent a similar
emotion. Despite his scholastic musings and his poetic dic-

tion, Stephen occasionally (if rarely) betrays his emotional needs: "Touch me. Soft eyes. Soft soft soft hand. I am lonely here. O, touch me soon, now. . . . I am quiet here alone. Sad too. Touch, touch me" (49). These very simple phrases indicate their insistence by their brevity and simplicity; without balance and order they are filled with emotion.

Bloom, older than Stephen, knows whether he is a father, but that is not to say that he knows about the mystery: "If little Rudy had lived. See him grow up. . . . Walking beside Molly in an Eton suit. My son. Me in his eyes. Strange feeling it would be. From me. Just a chance. Must have been that morning in Raymond terrace. . . . Give us a touch, Poldy. God, I'm dying for it. How life begins" (89). The exactness of place and time, morning at Raymond terrace, belies the mystery of how life really does begin, only giving it a local habitation and a name. Bloom is faced with not one but both of the two great mysteries of man: he must ask not only the questions of life but also of death. He tries to place himself in the center of the absence ("My son. Me in his eyes") so as to be as near the mystery of life and death as language can bring him.

Bloom thinks of how Richie Goulding dotes upon his daughter Crissie (whom Simon Dedalus, in his unique combination of wit and paternal insouciance, called "papa's little lump of dung"): "Still harping on his daughter. Wise child that knows her father, Dedalus said. Me?" (273). Unsure even of being the father of his own daughter —a suspicion current among his Dublin peers—Bloom is unsure of his own part in the intangible relationship of father and daughter. He phrases his feeling succinctly, in the terse manner of what we have called the inverse ratio (which shows what it means to him): "Me?" The self is present, clearly so, without pattern and thus free, but in a questioned and open position.

Through the haze of a style reminiscent of Lamb, the problem of paternity surfaces again in "Oxen":

> Now he is himself paternal and these about him might be his sons. Who can say? The wise father knows his own child. He thinks of a drizzling night in Hatch street, hard by the bonded stores there, the first. . . . They are entwined in nethermost darkness, the willer and the willed, and in an instant (*fiat!*) light shall flood the world. Did heart leap to heart? Nay, fair reader. . . . No, Leopold! . . . There is none now to be for Leopold, what Leopold was for Rudolph. (413–14)

The reciprocal balance of willer and willed, which is made of the patterns of both life and language, is not enough to insure creation; there is something less predictable, more mysterious behind it all. Light does not flood the world. There is a curt question, succinct amid the flow of Lamb's prose, which speaks it all: "Who can say?"

Language cannot say; free of pattern, it can only question and suggest for the characters through the gaps in its system which open to the infinite reaches of their emotions. As noted above, the words around which boundaries cannot be drawn are the emotions; and here is again Bloom's feeling about patterning: "Words? Music? No: it's what's behind" (274). Behind the pattern, even behind the words themselves, lies what is important.

Mere words are often not even signs for emotions. Listening to the seductive and kinetic music sung in the

Ormond Bar, Bloom says: "He bore no hate. Hate. Love. Those are names. Rudy. Soon I am old" (285). *Love* and *hate* here are grammatically (primarily typographically) balanced, counterpoised like the antonyms they are. In the case of the pair *plums* and *plumstones,* syntax makes easily parallel what are vastly separate things emotionally; here it only reiterates by its pattern what one takes to be true, an opposition of terms. But this is exactly what Bloom rejects, refusing to feel what the language demands: "Those are names," general terms whose specific meanings can never be captured by a simple designation. They are terms which are empty before the incontrovertible but incomprehensible fact of the lost son. Bloom talks of growing old, a process in nature which is orderly and sequential. Yet the language he uses does not represent that process (as with the entelechic sentences); rather he speaks in such a way as to leap around the tracks of linguistic patterns. He says, with studied ungrammaticality, "soon I am old," rather than the expected "I will be." It is again a quantum leap, a free flight that disdains the order of time and language.

Perhaps the peak of emotion behind language is reached in the climax of "Circe," just as the peak of language as union is reached in "Ithaca" in the phrase "theirhisnothis." Stephen's version of Yeats's "Fergus" poem has appeared in the very beginning of the novel as a mocking injunction from Mulligan for Stephen not to brood. The phrase "love's bitter mystery" becomes a motif attending Stephen's memories of his mother and his pain at her death. Whatever the poignant reasons for the poem's appeal to Stephen, it had a particular connotation for Joyce as a suggestion of the kind of feelings that can lie behind literary allusions. When Joyce's youngest brother George lay dying of peritonitis, Stanislaus recalls, "he asked Jim to sing for him the setting he had composed for Yeats's poem: 'Who will go drive with Fergus now, / And pierce the deep wood's woven shade?' Jim went downstairs to the parlour, and, leaving the doors open, sat down at the piano and sang the melancholy chant to which he had set the verses."[17] Joyce associated the poem with death, both in his own life and in his novel in connection with Stephen's mother. Biography, music, poetry, and especially the emotions which invest them are conveyed by the freedom of language, which, resonant if unclear, speaks to their mystery.

STEPHEN

(Murmurs.)
. . . shadows . . . the woods.
. . . white breast . . . dim . . .

· · ·

BLOOM

(Communes with the night.) Face reminds me of his poor mother. In the shady wood. The deep white breast. Ferguson, I think I caught. A girl. Some girl. Best thing could happen him . . . *(He murmurs.)* . . . swear that I will always hail, ever conceal, never reveal, any part or parts, art or arts . . . *(He murmurs.)* in the rough sands of the sea . . . a cabletow's length from the shore . . . where the tide ebbs . . . and flows . . .

(Silent, thoughtful, alert, he stands on guard, his fingers at his lips in the attitude of secret master. Against the dark wall a figure appears slowly, a fairy boy of eleven, a changeling, kidnapped, dressed in an

144

*Eton suit with glass shoes and a little bronze helmet,
holding a book in his hand. He reads from right to left
inaudibly, smiling, kissing the page).*

BLOOM

(Wonderstruck, calls inaudibly.) Rudy!

RUDY

*(Gazes unseeing into Bloom's eyes and goes on read-
ing, kissing, smiling. He has a delicate mauve face. On
his suit he has diamond and ruby buttons. In his free
left hand he holds a slim ivory cane with a violet bow-
knot. A white lambkin peeps out of his waistcoat
pocket.)* (609)

Bloom totally misunderstands Stephen's words, as if he
could not tell poetry from a cabbage: "The deep white
breast. Ferguson, I think I caught. A girl. Some girl. Best
thing could happen him" (609). Yet the misunderstanding
at the level of allusion, of literature, and even of language
is really a transcendent empathy of emotions beyond language (like Bloom's apprehension of his and Stephen's
mystery "not verbally. Substantially"). Bloom only appre-
hends the words, the nouns and adjectives, free and without order. They exist like the emotional qualities they
imitate. Validity is not in how a thing is said (its syntax),
but in what is said, and in what is behind the words.
Bloom answers Stephen's poetry with poetry of his own,
garbled, masonic, and borrowed; each phrase seems independent. Bloom's words are certainly no response to Stephen's: language here is clothed in mystery. The result,
however, is not two men speaking without effect into the
night, but rather coming together through and despite
language. One notes that Bloom is described as "com-
muning" with the night; the result of this communion,

paradoxically achieved, is Bloom's vision of his lost son, the son born in and taken by mystery.

The exaggerated figure of the child continues the sense of emotion behind language; he reads backwards, as if contrarily, silently, and incommunicatively (although the reading of Hebrew is also suggested). Bloom's response is fitting not only to this strange vision, but also to the sense of his deep emotions: *"(Wonderstruck, calls inaudibly)."* Yet Rudy goes on kissing the page, and in this gesture lies a key to the complex unease with language in *Ulysses.* Bloom is struck dumb by the vision and cannot find words to explain the mysteries of his life; yet it is language which brought him to the point at which he can see beyond.

The core of mystery and the relentless and unanswered questions which ordered language cannot solve and which free language must express persist until the end of the book. Molly lies in bed, Bloom asleep next to her, his feet to her face. As her thoughts move on and on they come back to Bloom as their focal point, the Bloom she has known for sixteen years and whom the reader has known for eighteen chapters, the Bloom who is himself a mystery. She thinks of their courtship (the companion piece in the freedom of language to Bloom's reverie in Byrne's pub): "he asked me to say yes and I wouldnt answer first only looked out over the sea and the sky I was thinking of so many things he didnt know of" (782). At the moment of their closest union there existed large areas of Molly's experience which she could hardly understand and Bloom knew nothing of, intellectual and spiritual mysteries again among the "hearts going like mad": "and then I asked him with my eyes to ask again yes and then he asked me would I yes to say yes." He asks, she asks him to ask, two individuals are interacting in the give-and-take alternation that embodies the physical form of all relationships; but they ask for answers to questions not explicitly asked, and ask questions not fully answered by language. The reply, Molly's repeated and impassioned *yes*, is the language of un-limited possibilities. Her language disdains all constraints and limits: punctuation, grammar, syntax. The reply is the affirmation of the spirit behind language, and of the language which frees that spirit. It is the fine counterbalance to Bloom's earlier *no*, the *no* which tried to stop the patterns of language's seemingly dispassionate determination. Bloom's *no* early in the day—"No. Not think"—and Molly's *yes* at the end are not contradictions, but are both parts of a language which is at the same time ordered and free.

The mystery that Joyce valued lies not only at the heart of each individual character, but also at the heart of language; and it would be impossible to say which of the two related mysteries takes prominence. It is clear that the mystery and integrity of the characters are expressed and preserved symbolically by the mystery of the appropriate order (that is to say disorder) of language that Joyce creates to allow for particular cases and unique expressions. It is not the word known to all men that is Joyce's concern in the expressive form of his language (if it is Stephen's query to his mother's ghost), it is rather the case that each man must have his word and that each man and each word are unique, sometimes to the point of complete inde-pendence.

For when Bloom stands inaudible and wonderstruck at the vision of his son, suddenly robbed of language before his great personal vision, the moment betrays a different ultimate direction of the free side of language for the char-

147

acters. Much of the communication between Bloom and Stephen, or that questioning between Bloom and Molly, is precariously poised between, on the one hand, misunderstanding and misuse of language and, on the other, non-understanding and no use at all. The contrariness of Rudy's reading in the wrong direction suggests this gradual approach to non-language.

The ultimate direction and end of a language that is free is a sort of linguistic chaos. Without order and form to adopt, language loses the lines that give it meaning and direction. The free language reaches, as it were, the limit of no limits. It makes sense only in contrast to patterns; but it seeks to undo itself by disdaining those patterns that make it any language at all. Moreover as it moves towards an individuation, it moves as well toward a plurality that admits of no general order. Wittgenstein correctly points out that boundaries cannot explain all the possible uses of language, but a progressive plurality without common ground and limit leads to an infinity of particulars. A calculus may be a tyranny, but no system at all may be chaos.

Joyce deliberately indulges in this tendency to absolute plurality, to minute particularity without the order of system, even to chaos. It has been observed that he counterbalances in dialectic tension one element of language with the other, order and appropriateness, and that he offsets the implications of each, physical and emotional; so in a similar manner he counterpoises the limits and bad excesses. Just as he shows the limits of the order of language as confining and trapping for the characters, so he demonstrates the limits of linguistic freedom as an uncertainty of infinite questions, limitless choice, and the chaos of non-language.

At the end of "Oxen of the Sun" the analogous processes of language and life reach their respective afterbirths. The fragments and phrases float, released from the linguistic chain of speaker and hearer, cut off from the patterns of semantics and syntax.

> Waiting guvnor? Most deciduously. Bet your boots on. Stunned like seeing as how no shiners is acoming, Underconstumble? He've got the chink *ad lib*. Seed near free poun on un a spell ago said war hisn. Us come right in on your invite, see? Up to you, matey. Out with the oof. Two bar and a wing. You larn that go off of they there Frenchy bilks? Won't wash here for nuts nohow. Lil chile vely solly. Ise de cutest colour coon down our side. Gawds teruth, Chawley. We are nae fou. We're nae tha fou. Au reservoir, Mossoo. Tanks you. (426)

It is a melange of dialects: southern Negro, "Ise de cutest"; Cockney English, "guvnor"; pidgin English, "Lil chile." There are other languages: Scots, "We're nae tha fou"; and French, "Au reservoir." All these build a plurality of particulars and a chaos of individual expressions that defies the train of communication and holds only tenuously to the order of syntax. Bloom is lost here: not speaking himself, he can follow neither the drift of the conversation nor the movement of the group. If patterns of language bound him tightly to what passed in life, the free can leave him behind. He has to run to catch up with Stephen.

The free language in *Ulysses* degenerates to a point where it is unrecognizable, without important syntactic order and clinging only to morphemic structure. In a subconscious vision, Bloom's grandfather Virag gives some

advice: "Hik! Hek! Hak! Hok! Huk! Kok! Kuk!" (521).
Bloom does not respond: there can be no answer to a
language of no linguistic meaning. Bloom imagines the
consummation of Blazes's and Molly's affair, an event
which is most disturbing and upsetting to him:

BOYLAN'S VOICE

(Sweetly, horsely, in the pit of his stomach.) Ah!
Gooblazqruk brukarchkrasht!

MARION'S VOICE

(Hoarsely, sweetly rising to her throat.) O! Weesh-
washtkissima pooisthnapoohuck! (567)

Language has nearly expired in this passage. It has been
reduced to mere sounds and letters on a page, perhaps
mimicking the action. There is no order, no rebellion from
it, and hence no verbal meaning.

These last examples point to the place where language
breaks all orders, where it undoes itself and ceases to be
language. At that point verbal art ceases to be. Yet Joyce
indulges the license of his language to that point of particularity and plurality in the text because it demonstrates
something at the level of the artist-figure. When Joyce
preserves the integrity of both his characters and his language he does so at the expense of the reader. Every word
that insists on its undeterminable particularity, every gap
that speaks a pregnant silence are only puzzles and mysteries that keep the text and characters inviolate from the
eager inquiries of the reader. Where thematic schemes,
structural plans, or syntactic patterns easily lead the
reader to a sense of several of the meanings of the text,
mystery, license, and syntactic silence only assert the intangible quality of the work and the artist-figure who cre-

ates it. There is always something unknown and even unknowable about the text and its words, and the reader is lead to search for some sign of the artist-figure, some glimpse of his face. He might even be led to ask the artist for the Word.

When the last questions in "Ithaca" ask with whom Bloom has traveled and when, the answers provide variety and multiple identity through the patterns of language:

> With?
> Sinbad the Sailor and Tinbad the Tailor and Jinbad
> the Jailer and Whinbad the Whaler and Ninbad the
> Nailer and Finbad the Failer and Binbad the Bailer
> and Pinbad the Pailer and Minbad the Mailer and
> Hinbad the Hailer and Rinbad the Railer and Din-
> bad the Kailer and Vinbad the Quailer and Linbad the
> Yailer and Xinbad the Phthailer.

Yet the studied effect of this patterned variety actually serves less to indicate characters than to present forcefully the single artist behind the constructions, the one who is responsible for creating the language. In the question immediately following he appears even more clearly:

> When?
> Going to a dark bed there was a square round
> Sinbad the Sailor roc's auk's egg in the night of the
> bed of all the auks of the rocs of Darkinbad the
> Brightdayler. (737)

This passage—loose, paratactic, even confusing—clearly attempts to point to the maker of the words, the unique artist. The example is evidently a particular product of a single creating source. Such particular constructions build

151

to an embarrassment of riches in the novel, and each *hapax legomenon* in the text shows the possibilities which the artist can create. What is plurality and variety at the level of the characters points to the unique individual expression of the artist.

There is a paradox lurking in this, one by now to be expected in the dialectics of Joyce's language. While the openness of language represents manifold identity and variety for the characters, it represents the work of the single artist. More paradoxically, while it expresses the emotions and the intellectual search for meaning of the characters, it represents the "body" of the artist. Each construction ultimately individuates the one who creates, the one who makes and manipulates every particular sentence, and it is the function of the body to individuate.

When the fixed patterns of language enact the physical world of the characters, what is figured for the artist is, because of the dialectic, in opposition to that: his mind and creative intelligence. Thus the dialectic allows us to extrapolate about the artist in terms opposite to those of the characters. When the freedom of language enacts for the characters their emotional and intellectual world, we can infer that the opposite in the dialectic, the body, is enacted for the artist. The expressive form of syntax allows us to speak, even if metaphorically, about the body of the artist because the syntax clearly reveals a unique, individual source of creation.

Joyce has taken his language to its limits in order to show the paradoxical relationship between the levels of artist and character. Just as he took the constructions of order to their determined limit to reveal the physical world of the novel and the intellectual power of the cre-

ator, so he takes the opened constructions to the limit of
plurality and intellectual ineffability for the characters so
as to reveal his unique self, the body of the artist.

That the artist creates with and from his body is a
metaphoric notion fundamental to Joyce. The statement
from Stephen's diary about the artistic endeavor to go
forth for the millionth time (used in this study as a means
of understanding the place of language in Joyce's art) con-
cerns the involvement of the external world with the inner
artist. The religious metaphors of creation in the *Portrait*
are turned to artistic ones: "the virgin womb of the imagination" (217) stresses the physical as well as the spiritual
side of the artist's work. In *Ulysses*, the theory that Stephen argues so earnestly in the library is based on the belief that what lies in art is what was within the artist. The
clearest statement that the body of the artist is the source
of his art is from *Finnegans Wake:*

> He shall produce nichthemerically from his unheaven-
> ly body a no uncertain quantity of obscene matter
> not protected by copriright in the United Stars of
> Ourania or bedeed and bedood and bedang and be-
> dung to him, with this double dye, brought to blood
> heat, gallic acid on iron ore, through the bowels of his
> misery, flashly, faithly, nastily, appropriately, this
> Esuan Menschavik and the first till last alshemist wrote
> over every square inch of the only foolscap available,
> his own body, till by its corrosive sublimation one
> continuous present tense integument slowly unfolded
> all marryvoising moodmoulded cyclewheeling history
> (thereby, he said, reflecting from his own individual
> person life unlivable, transaccidentated through the
> slow fires of consciousness into a dividual chaos, per-
> ilous, potent, common to allflesh, human only, mortal)
> but with each word that would not pass away the

> squidself which he had squirtscreened from the crys-
> talline world waned chagreenold and doriangrayer
> in its dudhud. (185–86)

The artist's body is not the only subject of his art but is also the substance of it: his corporeal identity is both message and medium. His very skin and blood, by the alchemy of art, become his paper and ink, and if he pares his fingernails in seeming indifference, it is only to use those products of his body as artistic material. In short, his body of art is his body, "faithly" and "appropriately."

From this view the artist who is supposed to disappear from his art never does. The appropriate freedom physically binds him to his art. In creating a variety of unique constructions, Joyce makes clear an expression of his own self: the freedom of his syntax is ultimately his attempt to assert the possibilities of language which are themselves an assertion of his very bodily being as a creator. In seeking a language less and less bound by general orders, more and more nearly unique, he seeks to assert his own person as artist. What he gestures towards is the construction of a language with an ontology of its own, an ontology which affirms his own being as an individually creating artist-figure.

Something akin to this is experienced by the young Stephen in his contact with the prostitute at the end of chapter 2 in the *Portrait:* "A vague speech . . . beyond sin or odor" (101). Stephen also experiences "a long liquid joy" which "flowed through the words" (226). For him, language has an existence of its own. Later in his life, Stephen continues to create this language of almost independent ontology: "Oomb, allwombing tomb"; "I am almosting it." He tries to write the sounds of wave speech, turning the products of his body into art: "a fourworded wavespeech: seesoo, hrss, rsseeiss, ooos" (49). Stephen's artistic quest for this living language has moved from "vague speech" to "wavespeech"; there might be an association by means of a suppressed pun in the two incidents (*vague* being French for wave). The connection between the two separate incidents, however, is in the direction of language beyond normal order and form, moving to a life of its own.

The creation of such a language has consequences which can turn against the artist. As the language moves beyond convention, it moves to an independence, an "almosting it," and in the variety of its own being lives less and less for the artist who made it. The independent ontology is an artistic success but one so rare as to erase the traces of the successful artist.

This is the point at which the freedom of language becomes difficult even for the artist. Not the chaos which threatens the characters with plurality, but rather the independence of language, so alive with its own being, threatens to sever connections with the controlling individual who made it. The language proceeds so far beyond any pattern and order as not to be recognizably part of the physical creator at all. As the physicality of individuation for the characters is ultimately undone by the general patterns of language used to express that very individuation, so is the body of the artist by the potential chaos of the free constructions which seek to portray that individuation. This is the limit of the free principle for the artist: language is almost independent of him.

Joyce points that far, to the ultimate nothingness beyond patterns and orders of language, to the chaos out of which new language arises, but he does not go there in *Ulysses*. Perhaps *Finnegans Wake* is the artistic attempt at a new independent language beyond the established orders, but *Ulysses* is firmly within that recognizable framework. It insists on the particular, the individual, and the ineffable, for both character and artist, but cannot disdain the order that also gives meaning to each. The novel is conceived within order and pattern, and the syntax which is so important a part of Joyce's appropriate order is itself necessary. It provides the free constructs with fibre and, as Lindley Murray says, sense. Within that order, the novel can both use language and abuse it, and with that order Joyce need not relinquish his control.

In literature we move through a blest world in which we know nothing except by style, but in which also everything is saved by it.   Henry James

Best value in Dublin.   *Ulysses*

6 Appropriate Order as Controlled Meaning

The control observed throughout the previous chapters in all the various contexts of syntax in dialectic is only the manifestation of the control Joyce exercises over syntax itself. "She had cut her [hair] that very morning on account of the new moon and it nestled about her pretty head in a profusion of luxuriant clusters and pared her nails, too, Thursday for wealth" (349). The enjambment of two parallel independent clauses—"she had cut" and "[she had] pared"—so close to the independent clause modifying hair by the paratactic *and* (not to speak of the run-on addition of Gerty's own homily at the end) results in a syntactic involution that suggests Gerty's hair as having an identity of its own, paring its nails as the artist-god is said to do, only far less indifferently. Nearly every sentence in the novel, in that it is subject to such appropriate ordering, is controlled very carefully and to a certain effect. That effect is more than comic, although it makes great allowances for irony and ambiguity, and it is far from the indifference of manicure, either cosmetic or artistic.

Hugh Kenner has observed, in reference to the quotation from "Nausicaa" above, that "Joyce's repertory of syntactic devices is not extensive."[1] That is true, but only

157

a part of the truth. Insofar as all of the uses of syntax are reducible to the basic opposition of order and appropriateness, the devices are hardly numerous. Yet the uses of those limited devices in the contexts of author and text, artist-figure and character, are manifold. If the principles constructing the syntax are few, the constructions are not: nearly every sentence in the novel is of a rather high frequency. Meaning is conveyed in the expressive form and dialectic principles of the syntax. As David Hayman notes, this meaning is understood "through the medium [in its formal aspects] and in terms of it";[2] and it is a meaning no less varied and cogent for its being expressed through a limited number of devices.

Yet the dialectical contexts behind the devices, as rich and suggestive as they can be made by association and analogy, are themselves ultimately all reducible to binary opposition: reality and experience meeting soul, or matter engaging mind, can be seen as a paradigm for almost any meaning. Joyce, however, was not engaged in a primarily intellectual construction, and he recognized that fact. Constantly aware of the limits of language, acknowledging the limitations of the artist, he also confessed to his limitations as a thinker. To Frank Budgen he admitted: "In my case the thought is always simple."[3]

The thought is simple because the control behind it is simple too. While both artist-figure and characters are engaged in the dialectic, there is a basic difference. The characters' entire lives are circumscribed, directed by processes and patterns, restricted by limits, and specifically controlled by the language created by the artist. That figure constantly exploits the limits of syntax so that its more threatening aspects operate at their level: the arbi-

trariness of order, the determinism is that order's entelechy, or the chaos of linguistic plurality. The characters
exist, but only through and in terms of the creativity of
the artist, through his control of language. He is free while
they are transfixed; he is creative, they contingent. The
artist-figure, not without irony but certainly with intent,
is free to control both the freedom and the appropriateness
of his constructions; his characters are always fixed and
controlled in both the order and the freedom of their constructed world.

It is by means of that control, through the counter-
balancing of their endeavor with his, that Joyce renders a
sense of conviction. Just as he gives sense and proportion
to his language by the control of syntax, so by the control
over the world of his characters in that language he imparts proportion and value to their lives. Joyce had to rely
on Murray's grammar in order to render meaningful his
own "order in every way appropriate": without linguistic
order to rebel against, his linguistic freedom had no meaning. Nietzsche recognized that there is a moral order inherent in the linguistic one: "I fear we are not getting rid
of God because we still believe in grammar."[4] Control over
characters, like control over language, is finally proportion,
harmony, and sense.

Not that Joyce ever wanted to get rid of God; he merely
wanted to supplant Him as the source of all control. The
artist-god in the text, as we have seen, is neither indifferent nor aloof. He is evident foremost in a language that
is first disruptive of the normal order of syntax and then
insistent on its own appropriate order. That language in
turn manifests him. Its system and patterns demonstrate
the creative power of his intellect, as he apportions, ranks,

and creates a functional system for his characters. He also can be seen in his maintenance of those systems; he constructs his sentences and projects them into the void where they appear to stop, supporting them, as Atlas does the world, through the connections of the order he utilizes. The entelechy of his sentences, the developing progress of his language, points back to the presence of the artist as a prime mover: initiating and directing the ordered motion of language. The opposite side of language, the freer, also manifests the artist. It engages his freedom to create a language of variety, that possibility arising from his exploitations of linguistic order; and the multiplicity of the constructions reveals the body of the particular creator. His activity is a freedom both to order and to disorder, and his self is increased by both. He does not stand above and beyond but rather is always *in* his art, creating it through language and being revealed, mind and body both, by that same language.

Any substantiation of God was important to Joyce: as First Cause or as Prime Mover, respectively, the two forms of the artist-figure in the text as creator of his own order and as the initiator of sentence movement and duration; and importantly as the Last Thing, the last court of appeal and the final word (Molly may utter it, but Joyce wrote it). In this capacity he is far from benign: his characters exact harsh penalties in the world created for them. It is a world undoubtedly ordered and ruled by a system. The form of an imperial government, that of the Catholic church, that of social custom, all represented by that of syntax, cabin, crib, and confine. The order within *Ulysses*, in its themes and language, is present because it represents for Joyce something that goes on in the world. Life for the

characters is lived in a sphere of constant limit, physical
and linguistic as well as moral, to go beyond whose pale
is not to live. Theirs is a world of bodily functions and
appetites. The character's physical existence, his very
body, is itself delineated by linguistic order. In the world
of the characters, events and circumstances hedge them
in; social and grammatical connections circumscribe their
movement. These are reflected in language by corresponding connections: men are united by language into a group,
and a matrimonial violator both exists with and makes
possible a "matrimonial violated." Life can be harsh for
the characters; it abuses Bloom with the facts of his son's
death and his wife's infidelity, and never lets him forget.
Language reflects that harsh order; through patterns seemingly determined, it suggests the realities he would wish
to avoid. The character's freedom of self-expression is
limited by what the patterns have described. Whether lov-
ing, thinking, or speaking, man is tied by the orders of
language as by life. It is the contingent character whom
Joyce portrays, the one who moves through words and
days that are essentially limited and controlled. Even the
artist-figure himself is similarly circumscribed by the order
he uses appropriately and not.

Joyce never relinquishes control over the least part of
his novel, from the details of its verisimilitude to the color
of its cover, and he exerts this control because he is concerned not only with what his art performs but also what
it conveys. In his long monologue on *Ulysses,* Jung apos-
trophied, "Du sagst nichts, und verrätst nichts, O Ulysses,
aber Du wirkst."[5] ("You say nothing, and you reveal nothing, O Ulysses, but you work an effect.") This is precisely
true: Joyce has constructed his medium so that it "works."

The final meaning of, syntax's appropriate order and expressive form comes from that source of control: it works to suggest a sense of Joyce's direction for and demonstration with his text. It is a sense of conviction, perhaps even of belief. Joyce seems only to have believed in himself, but as artist present within his text he creates a system whose dogma of dialectic is worthy of assent. Kenner notwithstanding, Joyce may have had a voice, one that speaks to the reader through the paradox of its order as God spoke to Moses through the paradox of the burning bush; or better, and less hyperbolic: if Joyce had more than one voice he still had something to convey. The sense of authorial judgment and conviction is usually attributed to authors far different from Joyce; yet the meaning of this book's syntax may stretch so far.

A description of life lived under patterns, controls, and limits, where people affect one another in ways not often noticed by themselves, could almost be a precis of a great social novel such as *Middlemarch*—the interinvolvement of Dr. Lydgate's plans, Bulstrode's pretenses, the lives of Mary Garth and Fred Vincy, Dorothea's realization of how she lives and has lived her life. George Eliot describes the world of her novel as follows:

> Old provincial society has its share of . . . subtle movement: had not only its striking downfalls, its brilliant young professional dandies who ended by living up an entry with a drab and six children for their establishment, but also those less marked vicissitudes which are constantly shifting the boundaries of social intercourse, and begetting new consciousness of interdependence. Some slipped a little downward, some got higher . . . and perhaps found themselves surprisingly grouped in consequence; while a few personages or

families that stood with rock firmness amid all this
fluctuation, were slowly representing new aspects in
spite of solidity, and altering with the double change
of self and beholder. Municipal town and rural parish
gradually made fresh threads of connection . . . , while
squires and baronets, and even lords who had once
lived blamelessly afar from the civic mind, gathered
the faultiness of closer acquaintanceship. Settlers, too,
came from distant countries, some with an alarming
novelty of skill, others with an offensive advantage in
cunning. In fact, much the same sort of movement
and mixture went on in old England as we find in
older Herodotus.[6]

Joyce is no less concerned with the texture of human society than Eliot. Their interests and focus within the novel
are the same: the connections, interdependence, rise and
fall of characters. Only Joyce's way is to enact this through
the language: he replicates the characters' struggles in the
expressive form of his syntax.

If Eliot and Joyce thus share the same concern at the
level of the characters in the text, one nevertheless considers Eliot as more of a moralist; her narrator comments
judiciously on the follies and fears of the characters and
offers a corrective to their level of existence. When Mr.
Casaubon founds his baseless hope for a marital future on
"his long and studious bachelorhood [that] had stored up
for him a compound interest of enjoyment," the narrator
comments by way of correcting his ignorant exuberance:
"We all of us, . . . get our thoughts entangled in metaphors, and act fatally on the strength of them."[7] This is
what one expects from the artist in the nineteenth-century
novel: ethical comment and criticism. Yet Joyce also comments on what passes at the level of the characters in the

text. His way, however, as with that presentation of the life of the novel, is through the dialectic of his syntactic constructions. The meaning of the particular form of syntax employed, opposite at the level of the artist to its meaning at the level of the character, acts as a corrective to the excesses of the text: it passes judgment on it. When Bloom seems trapped by the language he uses to describe events ("was that when he she?"), when he is threatened by language's tyranny, his fear and helplessness are counterbalanced and put into perspective by what is revealed at the level of the artist. In that context there is no tyranny, no confinement into a tightened world, but rather the benign power of the artist's ordering (the "he" and "she"), his capacity to exercise his creative potential through patterns. Similarly, as Bloom asserts his spirit and faces the void of ineffable life and its mystery, the artist bodily appears in the void. Indeed one could say that each and every event in the text, presented dialectically by a principled language, offers a corresponding comment on the characters at the level of the artist. Joyce and Eliot may not be so very far apart after all.

For all of Joyce's modern use of language (indeed precisely because of it), Joyce's world view may be closer in spirit to the novel of the nineteenth century than to that of the twentieth. Ezra Pound, growing in impatience and intolerance as the twentieth century progressed, would claim in his disillusionment that Joyce "had no philosophy, not so you would notice it . . . [only] some ruck end of theology and VERY conventional outlook."[8] Pound was not far off the mark; he may have even hit it. But it is the means by which Joyce expresses his view that is both striking and unconventional. A comparison with a self-confessed moralist of the twentieth century, D. H. Lawrence, is not at all to Joyce's discredit as a moralist.

Lawrence, according to the judgment of F. R. Leavis, is significant because of the human awareness he promotes, "awareness of the possibilities of life." In order to be part of a great tradition, a writer must have "an unusually developed interest in life."[9] That interest, a concern for the problems and the issues of being, is motivated by a kind of religious experience. As Lawrence notes in a letter to Edward Garnett, "Primarily I am a religious man."[10]

Lawrence's ethical feeling finds expression in art in what Leavis calls the "affirmation of norms."[11] These norms can be said to be presented in two ways. One is often loquacious exhortation of the reader in sermonlike pronouncements which string parts of the works together. The other is dramatic presentation: confrontation of characters who represent and express varied views, the validity of which is tested in the life of the novel. In these confrontations within the text one critic recognizes the "normative value of [Lawrence's] dramatized distinctions."[12]

The preachy pronouncements of Lawrence are troublesome and hardly a fair point of comparison. In the dramatic quality of the text, however, Leavis finds the union of idea and art, and this he contrasts with Joyce: "We have on the one hand the technical originality of the creations, and on the other their organic wholeness and vitality. But the critic who cannot see a marvel of form, of significant organization . . . finds the creative originality that really matters in the contrivances of Joyce, where insistent will and ingenuity so largely confess the failure of creative life."[13] Leavis believes that there is a moral function in the form of Lawrence's art, while Joyce's art is mere contrivance, and this is, to some extent, a frequent judgment. It was the supposed lack of morality in Joyce's aesthetic forms that brought down the thunder of Lawrence himself, who felt that attention to small points of aesthetic choice was morbid. Flaubert, for Lawrence inseparably linked with Joyce as a certain kind of artist, "stood away from life as from a leprosy."[14] His comment on Joyce is equally definite (and shows a cloacal obsession almost as great as the Irishman's): "My God, what a clumsy *olla putrida* Joyce is!"[15]

An immediate response to these charges is provided by the text of *Ulysses* itself with its syntax as a register of meaning. As has been shown in this study, language, in its expressive form and in the art which that creates, was not for Joyce a means to remove himself from life, but rather the means to enter most fully into a life both imaginative and natural. Art in the form Joyce gives it is analogous to and inseparable from life. Thus Lawrence is mistaken in pointing exclusively to Flaubert as Joyce's mentor; Aristotle is as much his model (see chapter 4), and Aristotle did indeed speak for life. The careful structuring of language in the balance of order and freedom is not aloof aestheticism; it yields not objective constructs, but often subjective ones. The creation of art involves a moral choice because Joyce's language acts out and judges the life which is its subject and model. Through the careful ordering of the dialectic within his dual language Joyce expresses both the plan and the puzzle of life.

Ironically, even a little perversely, Lawrence's desire for an integral being, for a wholeness of personality, is fulfilled by Joyce's dialectic in language. Lawrence's concept of a harmonious self was characterized, in Spilka's

166

words, by principles "at odds in [a character's] psychology," these being "balance and excess, wholeness and partness, sustenance and reduction." Lawrence "called for a balance of elements . . . will, sympathy, spirit, flesh and intellect."[16] But emotion and intellect, body and mind are the substance of the dialectic in which Joyce engages through the particular constructions of his principled language. What Lawrence felt must be articulated by the characters within the work is enacted by the language of Joyce's text, and to a more integral effect. There is no need for the artist to make moral pronouncements when the language itself speaks.

In addition, the entelechy embodied in certain of Joyce's constructed sentences represents a profound statement in favor of life. The incomplete sentences generate their own ends, growing from what exists inherently within them. This growth at the level of syntax, the development and coming-to-be of meaning, is not merely a metaphor but actually imparts a corresponding sense of development and growth to the material it treats: the characters, plot, world of the novel. The entelechic sentences are the analogue of life; they involve a growth which is truly organic —and here the sentences show their Aristotelian origin. Going Lawrence one better, many sentences in Joyce "speak for life" and for possibilities of life as it grows into what it will become. "A paper. He liked to read at stool. Hope no ape comes knocking just as I'm" (67). The last part of this sentence will develop into something dictated by syntactic laws which direct its movement and growth. It is as organic as its subject matter, Bloom in the outhouse. Language is at all levels truly natural.

Lawrence's sentences are similar to Joyce's in being inwardly moved and directed. Lawrence builds his sentences by subtle (and often not so subtle) repetition with slight variation in order to give a sense of increased intensity and movement toward some fulfillment. Yet that fulfillment, like the sexual climax it seeks to emulate, is often not attained. The reason for this breaking off, according to Harry Moore, lies in "Lawrence's dynamism; his avoidance of the static."[17] But this avoidance often has a result that Lawrence would not wish. In a crucial encounter between Gerald and Gudrun, their death-haunted love is consummated with the following description: "His brain was hurt, seared, the tissue was as if destroyed. He had not known how hurt he was, how his tissue, the very tissue of his brain was damaged by the corrosive flood of death. Now, as the healing lymph of her effluence flowed through him, he knew how destroyed he was, like a plant whose tissue is burst from inwards by a frost."[18] The simplicity and iteration of a verb, adjective, and noun give a sense of hammering intensity. The vocabulary veers from concrete (*brain, tissue*) to abstract (*effluence*). Yet despite its seeming realism, the text presents little directly; rather it uses similes ("as if destroyed," "like a flower") and metaphor ("flood of death"). Actual natural terms are also used metaphorically (*lymph*). The reality portrayed is thus largely illusionary. Similarly one's expectation of an end is disappointed. The sentence structure seems to progress, but the sense of questioning, the repeated *how*, leads to no answer. The nouns are elaborated but not developed; appositives turn on themselves: "his tissue, the very tissue." The result is a sense of a blind impulse, a thrust without direction. The passage is without commitment, without a definitive

168

end; it could even be accused of ultimately standing off
from the life it seems to portray, by evasion, misdirection,
metaphor.

The sense of wholeness, integrity, and completion which
Lawrence advocated seems somehow unattained by his
text, if this example stands up to extrapolation. Joyce, on
the other hand, seemingly aesthetic and aloof, writes sentences which represent a sense of value in the world
they describe, which enact in their dialectic Lawrence's
desired wholeness of being, and which in their syntax
carry the seeds of their own growth. It is Joyce who has
achieved the combination of idea and art that Leavis
claimed for Lawrence. The vision and the form of Joyce's
art are one: his artistic choices suggest moral ones, and
his moral perspective (albeit simple) informs his aesthetic
view. Joyce's style is organic in a sense even beyond what
Lawrence understood by it; in a linguistic sense it is organic in being the union of form and content.[19] It is a consummation such as Lawrence might have devoutly wished:
a marriage fertile both for art and for the meaning which
that art fosters.

Yet if it is an art which Lawrence only promised and
Joyce delivered, it is an art whose interest in order and
appropriate variations of it makes it relish control. The
final paradox among so many created and exploited by
the novel is the fact that while the language of *Ulysses* is
the most original in technique of the twentieth century, the
themes and the meaning that the language enacts are
the substance of the nineteenth. Joyce's mind and body
may have been on the continent—in Trieste, Zurich, and
postwar Paris—when he wrote the book, but his heart and

spirit were in Dublin; the reality of his artistic experience was in the future, but his soul was in the past. The puzzling meaning of *Ulysses*, the essential sense of so complex a text, is not solved but only ably served by the appropriate order of its syntax.

Notes

1 Joycean Syntax as Appropriate Order

1. James Joyce, *Ulysses* (New York, 1961), p. 644. All subsequent references in this study are to this edition and will be cited in the text.

2. *Letters,* ed. Stuart Gilbert and Richard Ellmann, 1:167.

3. Erwin R. Steinberg, "Characteristic Sentence Patterns in 'Proteus' and 'Lestrygonians,'" in Fritz Senn, ed., *New Light on Joyce from the Dublin Symposium,* p. 81.

4. A. Walton Litz, *The Art of James Joyce; James Joyce Quarterly* 12 (1974–75), nos. 1–2, "Textual Studies Issue"; and especially Michael Groden, *"Ulysses" in Progress.*

5. Steinberg, "Characteristic Sentence Patterns"; Liisa Dahl, *Linguistic Features of the Stream-of-Consciousness Techniques of James Joyce, Virginia Woolf and Eugene O'Neill.*

6. Reprinted in Herbert Gorman, *James Joyce,* p. 152.

7. *The Making of "Ulysses,"* p. 20.

8. Several works specifically focusing on Joyce's language have reached similar conclusions, although they do not pursue the consequences and meaning of Joyce's unique style. Liisa Dahl, in a summary article "The Linguistic Presentation of the Interior Monologue in Joyce's *Ulysses," James Joyce Quarterly* 7 (1970), observes succinctly, p. 119: "It seems evident that Joyce did not break too many rules at a time. If he chose strange vocabulary or new words his syntax was to a certain extent conventional." Robert Di Pietro, "A Transformational Note on a Few Types of Joycean Sentences," *Style* 3 (1969): 156–67: "Our premise is that most, if not all, sentences in Joyce's *Ulysses* lie within the grammatical confines of English and that his style consists, in no small part, of manipulations in the underlying tree structure."

9. Anthony Burgess, *Joysprick*, p. 76, describes the semantics of this sentence as calling for " 'laved', not washed, in this ceremony-of-innocence." He claims further that *"pale naked body* would not do" but does not say why. It would not do because Joyce's syntax, as it is here contended, is built up of such necessary lexical scrambling.

10. Two recent studies of Joyce's language have other views. Marilyn French, in *The Book as World*, suggests that the plurality of the separate styles of each chapter combines into a unified authorial view. Hugh Kenner, *Joyce's Voices*, claims that language, primarily through tone and diction, has an objective and independent ontology.

11. Litz, *The Art of James Joyce*, p. 35: "Principles which governed his work in 1920 and 1921 did not differ greatly from those he followed in writing *Finnegans Wake.*" These principles are largely thematic and technical, however; a glance at David Hayman's *First Draft Version of Finnegans Wake* (Austin: Univ. of Texas Press, 1963), shows how close the original *Finnegans Wake* was to lexical comprehension. Strother B. Purdy, in an ambitious article, "Mind Your Genderous: Toward a Wake Grammar," in Senn, *New Light on Joyce,* claims that even in *Finnegans Wake* the syntax "is the same as that of conventional English" (p. 47). Purdy states that a grammar of the *Wake* could be drawn within the general boundaries of transformational grammar. I discuss in chap. 2 the inadequacy of a transformational model as a description of the language of *Ulysses.*

12. For the issue of norms and deviations, see Levin, "Internal and External Deviations in Poetry," *Word* 21 (1965): 225–37.

13. "Aus dem Nachlass der Achtzigerjahre," *Werke in drei Bänden,* ed. Karl Schlecta (Munich: Hanser Verlag, n.d.), 3:86.

14. *My Brother's Keeper*, p. 108.

15. See Litz, *Art of James Joyce*, p. 39: "Joyce needed as many formal orders as possible to encompass and control his work."

16. Published in Richard Ellmann, *James Joyce*, p. 207.

17. Quoted in Ellmann, *James Joyce*, p. 129, p. 124.

18. Kevin Sullivan, *Joyce Among the Jesuits,* p. 76.

19. *Ibid.,* p. 76.

20. *Critical Writings,* ed. Ellsworth Mason and Richard Ellmann, p. 27.

21. *Letters,* 2:86.

22. *James Joyce,* p. 410.

23. *Letters,* 3:146.

24. See chap. 2 for an incidental use of Saussure in *Ulysses.*

25. See David Hayman, "Language Of / As Gesture" in *"Ulysses," cinquante ans après,* ed. L. Bonnerot, pp. 209–21; also Stephen Heath, "Ambiviolences," pp. 22–42, 64–77. Ellmann, *James Joyce,* p. 647, places the dates of the lectures in 1931.

26. Padraic and Mary Colum, *Our Friend James Joyce,* p. 131.

27. Stephen: "So that gesture, not music, not odours, would be a universal language, the gift of tongues rendering visible not the lay sense but the first entelechy, the structural rhythm" (p. 432).

2 Syntax: Principles and Contexts of Dialectic

1. Ludwig Wittgenstein, *Philosophische Grammatik* (Oxford, Basil Blackwell, 1969), p. 131. See also David A. White, "Joyce and Wittgenstein," *James Joyce Quarterly* 12 (1975): 294–304. White attempts "to correlate Wittgenstein's philosophical vision with Joyce's literary technique" and sees the philosopher's change of view on language as similar to Joyce's art developing towards the language of *Finnegans Wake.*

2. Di Pietro, "Transformational Note," pp. 159–60.

3. *My Brother's Keeper,* p. xix. The remark was made in response to his question about the impending threat of fascism.

4. *Der Zauberberg* (Frankfort: Fischer Verlag, 1967), p. 169.

5. *Language, Thought and Reality,* ed. John B. Carroll (Cambridge: M.I.T. Press, 1971), p. 58.

6. *Dublin's Joyce,* p. 12. In his most recent book, *Joyce's Voices,* language has a status of its own.

7. P. 2.

8. See Darcy O'Brien, *The Conscience of James Joyce.*

9. See Edwin R. Steinberg, *The Stream of Consciousness and Beyond in "Ulysses."*

10. Joyce, *A Portrait of the Artist as a Young Man* (New York, 1963), p. 253. All subsequent references, cited in the text, are to this edition.

11. See Ellmann, *Ulysses on the Liffey*, p. 86: "The pursuit of the ideal by Russell, or of the all-too-real by Mulligan, is wrong because it isolates. Solid earth must be transfused with liquid soul, here-and-now with timeless-placelessness." S. L. Goldberg, *The Classical Temper*, p. 64, sees Stephen's theory of artistic expression as one which can explain how "subject and object, meaning and quiddity, feeling and fact, are *fused* by the artist in his very medium, language."

12. See Jonathan Culler, *Structuralist Poetics* (Ithaca: Cornell Univ. Press, 1975), p. 225 on the procedure of extrapolation; citing Roland Barthes, Culler claims, "If the text presents two items . . . in a way to suggest opposition, then 'a whole space of substitution and variation' is open to the reader. . . . One can pass from one opposition to another . . . even inverting them."

13. *James Joyce*, p. 4.

14. See Ellmann, *James Joyce*, p. 565; Marshall McLuhan, "James Joyce: Trivial and Quadrivial," *Thought* 28 (1953): 75–98. This argument is most often put forward with reference to *Finnegans Wake.*

15. See also R. Jakobson, "Linguistics and Poetics," reprinted in Seymour Chatman, *Essays on the Language of Literature* (Boston: Houghton Mifflin, 1967), pp. 296–322. For a consideration of *Ulysses* in these terms, cf. Robert Scholes, "*Ulysses:* A Structuralist Perspective," pp. 161–71.

3 Order as Patterns

1. *Art of James Joyce*, p. 27.
2. *Making of "Ulysses,"* p. 21.

3. *Pound / Joyce,* ed. Forrest Read, p. 250.

4. *Language, Thought and Reality,* p. 73.

5. M. D. Berlitz, *First Book for Teaching Modern Languages* (Berlin: Cronbach, 1907), p. 14.

6. Cf. Hayman, "Language," pp. 214–15: "Joyce is not so much describing an event as reenacting it." Hayman sees this reenactment being achieved by "a combination of sounds, rhythms and attitudes."

7. Di Pietro, "Transformational Note," p. 162.

8. *James Joyce's "Ulysses,"* p. 208.

9. Budgen, *Making of "Ulysses,"* p. 16.

10. See Fritz Senn, "Book of Many Turns" in *"Ulysses" After Fifty Years,* ed. Thomas F. Staley (Bloomington: Univ. of Indiana Press, 1974), p. 34: "If we can parse [Bloom], we can parse humanity."

11. "Everyone eats in the *Odyssey* and everyone (except, perhaps, the Cyclops) offers everyone else something to eat." Howard W. Clark, *The Art of the "Odyssey,"* (Englewood Cliffs: Prentice-Hall, 1967), p. 14.

12. *James Joyce,* p. 383.

13. "The Text of *Ulysses,*" in Senn, *New Light on Joyce,* p. 105.

14. *Philosophische Grammatik,* pp. 130, 125.

4 Potential Order as Entelechy

1. See Burgess, *Joysprick,* p. 78, where he treats this sentence as an example of Joyce's "economy."

2. "Style and Its Image" in *Literary Style: A Symposium,* ed. Chatman (New York: Oxford Univ. Press, 1971), p. 6.

3. *James Joyce's "Ulysses,"* p. 255.

4. Aristotle, *Physica,* 201a10, 19915, *Works,* ed. W. D. Ross (Oxford: Clarendon Press, 1930), vol. 2.

5. *Metaphysica,* 1050a10–15, *Works,* vol. 8. The term *entelechy* in this chapter is interchangeable with the term *actuality* used in this quotation; this change is done with the purpose of

uniting Joyce's own terms with his method. This exchange of terms is not incorrect; cf. Aristotle: " 'actuality' is derived from 'action,' and points to the complete reality" (that is, the entelechy), *Metaphysica*, 1050a20. *Entelechy* was a term Aristotle applied equally to the physical sensible processes, as well as to the metaphysical ones; see below for further discussion on the switch from physical to metaphysical.

6. *Metaphysica*, 1050a30.

7. Arnold Goldman, *The Joyce Paradox*, chap. 4, makes several valuable points in this context; he notes how important movement and change are to meaning in the novel; for a fuller discussion of Joyce's use of Aristotle, see Jacques Aubert, *Introduction à l'esthétique de James Joyce*, especially chap. 3.

8. *Aristotle: Fundamentals of the History of His Development*, trans. R. Robinson (Oxford: Clarendon Press, 1934), pp. 380–85.

9. *Making of "Ulysses,"* p. 21.

10. Goldman, *Joyce Paradox*, p. 83.

11. *Language, Thought and Reality*, pp. 236, 242, 238, 147, 145.

12. Budgen, *Making of "Ulysses,"* p. 49.

13. Bloom, no deep thinker himself, comes to recognize motion in these two different ways. Early in the day he sees the physical motion of the planets as merely repetitive: "Gasballs spinning about, crossing each other, passing. Same old dingdong always" (167). By the evening he treats motion in another dimension: "And time? Well that's the time the movement takes" (374).

14. See Fritz Senn, "Esthetic Theories," *James Joyce Quarterly* 2 (1965): 134–36.

15. *Art of James Joyce*, p. 56. He considers only the "linear motion" of language.

16. Burgess, *Joysprick*, chap. 6, "Musicalisation," sees the temporality achieved wholly by the musical form.

17. *Aristotle* (New York: Dover, 1955), p. 58.

18. *Aristotle: Fundamentals*, p. 201.

19. See Haskell M. Block, "Theory of Language in Flaubert

and Joyce," *Revue de Littérature Comparée,* 25 (1961): 197–206.

20. Note how Stephen brings up a similar point when he discusses Shakespeare, the one after God who has created most: "But, because loss is his gain, he passes on towards eternity in undiminshed personality, untaught by the wisdom he has written or by *the laws he has revealed*" (*Ulysses,* 197, emphasis added).

21. Ellmann, *Ulysses on the Liffey,* p. 21.

22. G.W.F. Hegel, "Introduction to the Philosophy of History," in *The Modern Tradition,* ed. Ellmann and Feidelson (New York: Oxford Univ. Press, 1965), p. 459.

23. Stephen thinks that this is Aristotelian: "God: noise in the street: very peripatetic" (186). He probably makes an arbitrary association between walking in the streets and in the academy.

24. "James Joyce," reprinted in *Pound / Joyce,* p. 136.

5 Appropriate Freedom and Variety

1. *Conversations with James Joyce,* p. 74.

2. Wittgenstein, *The Blue and Brown Books* (New York: Harper and Row, 1965), from the *Blue Book,* p. 18.

3. This point has often been made; for example, see David Hayman, *"Ulysses": The Mechanics of Meaning,* p. 85: "Everything conspires to distract us from the characters' dilemmas, effectively limiting their viability as individuals."

4. Recounted in Ellmann, *James Joyce,* p. 538.

5. *Letters,* 2:49.

6. Colum, *Our Friend James Joyce,* p. 37.

7. *My Brother's Keeper,* p. 80.

8. See Clive Hart, "Joyce's Sentimentality," *Philological Quarterly,* 44 (1967): 516–26, for a thoughtful discussion of how Joyce's almost maudlin sentimentality was given fibre and irony by the density of language and form (this another variation on the dialectic of Joyce's art).

9. Among others, two occurrences of this phrase in *Ulysses* are at p. 16, when Stephen is thinking of his mother, and p. 243, when he confronts his sister at the booksellers.

10. John O. Lyons, "The Man in the MacIntosh" in *James Joyce Miscellany: Second Series,* ed. Marvin Magalaner, sees M'Intosh as Duffy in "A Painful Case" from *Dubliners* and claims that both he and Bloom are the "outcasts at life's feast."

11. Notesheets, British Museum MS 49975, "Nausicaa," p. 33/34 (Litz's numbers).

12. See Ellmann, *James Joyce,* p. 371, "Joyce knew . . . and moreover he believed that every human soul was unique."

13. *The Blue Book,* p. 27: "Philosophy, as we use the word, is a fight against the fascination which forms of expression exert upon us."

14. *The Blue Book,* p. 22: "There are certainly cases in which we say, 'I feel a longing, though I don't know what I'm longing for.' . . . Now we may describe these cases by saying that we have certain sensations not referring to objects. . . . In characterizing such sensations . . . these verbs will be intransitive."

15. Notesheets, British Museum, "Ithaca," p. 66 (Litz's numbering).

16. See Robert Boyle, "Mystery in *Ulysses,*" in Bonnerot, *"Ulysses," cinquante ans après,* pp. 243–61. Father Boyle claims that Joyce placed a "basic value" on mystery and portrayed both the religious mystery of the trinity and what Boyle calls "a human mystery which is analogous to the theological one."

17. *My Brother's Keeper,* p. 134.

6 Appropriate Order as Controlled Meaning

1. *Joyce's Voices,* p. 20.
2. *"Ulysses": The Mechanics of Meaning,* p. 17.
3. *The Making of "Ulysses,"* p. 284.
4. Cited in Jonathan Culler, *Structuralist Poetics* (Ithaca: Cornell Univ. Press, 1975), p. 96.

5. *"Ulysses:* Ein Monolog," *Anwendungen und Fortschritte der neueren Psychologie* (Zürich: Rascher Verlag, 1947), p. 169.

6. *Middlemarch* (Baltimore: Penguin Books, 1965), book 1, chap. 11, pp. 122–23.

7. *Ibid.*, chap. 10, p. 111.

8. *Pound / Joyce*, p. 268. Cf. Lionel Trilling, "James Joyce in his Letters," in William Chace, ed., *Joyce: A Collection of Critical Essays*, p. 165: "The ethos and mythos of the 19th century could still command from him some degree of assent." (One might say more than *assent.*)

9. *The Great Tradition* (New York: New York Univ. Press, 1967), pp. 2, 8.

10. *Letters of D. H. Lawrence* (London: Heinemann, 1932), p. 190.

11. *D. H. Lawrence: Novelist* (New York: Simon and Schuster, 1969), p. 69.

12. Mark Spilka, introduction to *D. H. Lawrence: A Collection of Critical Essays* (Englewood Cliffs: Prentice-Hall, 1963), p. 5.

13. *D. H. Lawrence: Novelist*, p. 27.

14. Quoted by Leavis, *The Great Tradition*, p. 8.

15. Quoted by William Deakin, "D. H. Lawrence's Attacks on Proust and Joyce," *Essays in Criticism* 7 (1957): 396.

16. *The Love Ethic of D. H. Lawrence* (Bloomington: Univ. of Indiana Press, 1971), pp. 9–10.

17. *"The Plumed Serpent:* Vision and Language," in *D. H. Lawrence: A Collection of Critical Essays*, p. 66.

18. *Women in Love* (New York: Modern Library, 1950), chap. 24, "Death and Love," p. 394.

19. Nils Enkvist, "On the Place of Style in Some Linguistic Theories," in *Literary Style: A Symposium*, ed. Seymour Chatman (New York: Oxford Univ. Press, 1971), p. 50: "the 'organic' view of style—the insistence on the inseparable unity of content or meaning and surface form."

Bibliography

By Joyce

Critical Writings. Ed. Ellsworth Mason and Richard Ellmann. New York: Viking Press, 1964.

Dubliners. New York: Viking Press, 1965.

Finnegans Wake. New York: Viking Press, 1965.

Letters. 3 vols. Ed. Stuart Gilbert and Richard Ellmann. New York: Viking Press, 1966.

Notesheets. British Museum MS 49975.

A Portrait of the Artist as a Young Man. New York: Viking Press, 1963.

Ulysses. New York: Random House, 1961.

Ulysses: A Facsimile of the Manuscript. Ed. Harry Levin and Clive Driver. New York: Octagon Books, 1975.

About Joyce

Adams, Robert M. *Surface and Symbol: The Consistency of James Joyce's "Ulysses."* New York: Oxford Univ. Press. 1962.

Aubert, Jacques. *Introduction à l'esthétique de James Joyce.* Etudes anglaises 46. Paris: Didier, 1973.

Blackmur, R. P. *Eleven Essays on the Modern Novel.* New York: Harcourt, Brace and World, 1964.

Blamires, Harry. *The Bloomsday Book: A Guide Through Joyce's "Ulysses."* London: Methuen, 1966.

Block, Haskell M. "Theory of Language in Flaubert and Joyce." *Revue de Littérature Comparée* 35 (1961): 197–206.

Bonnerot, L., ed. *"Ulysses," cinquante ans après.* Paris: Didier, 1974.

Budgen, Frank. *James Joyce and the Making of "Ulysses."* Bloomington: Univ. of Indiana Press, 1973.

Burgess, Anthony. *Joysprick: An Introduction to the Language of James Joyce.* London: André Deutsch, 1973.

————. *Rejoyce.* New York: Ballantine Books, 1966.

Chace, William, ed. *James Joyce: A Collection of Critical Essays.* Englewood Cliffs: Prentice-Hall, 1974.

Change 11. "L'atelier d'écriture" (Joyce issue). Ed. Jean Paris. Paris: Editions Seghers / Laffont, 1972.

Chatman, Seymour. "New Ways of Analyzing Narrative Structure, with an Example from Joyce's *Dubliners.*" *Language and Style* 2 (1968): 3–36.

Cixous, Hélène. *The Exile of James Joyce.* Trans. Sally A. J. Purcell. New York: D. Lewis, 1972.

Colum, Padraic and Mary. *Our Friend James Joyce.* New York: Doubleday, 1958.

Cope, Jackson I. "James Joyce: A Test Case for a Theory of Style." *English Literary History* 21 (1954): 221–36.

Curran, C. P. *James Joyce Remembered.* New York: Oxford Univ. Press, 1968.

Dahl, Liisa. *Linguistic Features of the Stream-of-Consciousness Techniques of James Joyce, Virginia Woolf and Eugene O'Neill.* Annales Universitatis Turkensis, Series B. Tom. 116. Turku: Turn Yliopisto, 1970.

Daiches, David. *The Novel in the Modern World.* Chicago: Univ. of Chicago Press, 1965.

Di Pietro, Robert. "A Transformational Note on a Few Types of Joycean Sentences." *Style* 3 (1969): 156–66.

Ellman, Richard. *The Conscience of Joyce.* New York: Oxford Univ. Press, 1977.

————. *James Joyce.* New York: Oxford Univ. Press, 1965.

————. *Ulysses on the Liffey.* New York: Oxford Univ. Press, 1973.

Evans, William. "Wordagglutinations in Joyce's *Ulysses.*" *Studies in the Literary Imagination* 3 (1970): 27–36.

French, Marilyn. *The Book as World.* Cambridge: Harvard Univ. Press, 1976.

182

Gifford, Don, and Robert Seideman. *Notes for Joyce: An Annotation of James Joyce's "Ulysses."* New York: Dutton, 1974.

Gilbert, Stuart. *James Joyce's "Ulysses."* New York: Random House, 1952.

Givens, Seon. *James Joyce: Two Decades of Criticism.* Augmented Edition. New York: Vanguard Press, 1963.

Goldberg, S. L. *The Classical Temper: A Study of James Joyce's "Ulysses."* New York: Barnes and Noble, 1961.

Goldman, Arnold. *The Joyce Paradox: Form and Freedom in His Fiction.* Evanston: Northwestern Univ. Press, 1966.

Gorman, Herbert. *James Joyce.* New York: Rinehart, 1948.

Groden, Michael. *"Ulysses" in Progress.* Princeton: Princeton Univ. Press, 1977.

Hanley, Miles L., ed. *A Word Index to James Joyce's "Ulysses."* Madison: Univ. of Wisconsin Press, 1951.

Hardy, Barbara. "Form As Ends and Means in *Ulysses." Orbis Litterarum* 19 (1964): 194–200.

Hart, Clive. "James Joyce's Sentimentality." *Philological Quarterly* 44 (1967): 516–26.

Hart, Clive, and David Hayman. *James Joyce's "Ulysses": Critical Essays.* Berkeley: Univ. of California Press, 1974.

Hayman, David. *Joyce et Mallarmé.* Paris: Lettres Modernes, 1956.

———. *"Ulysses": The Mechanics of Meaning.* Englewood Cliffs: Prentice-Hall, 1970.

Heath, Stephen. "Ambiviolences: Notes pour une lecture de James Joyce." *Tel Quel* 50–51 (1972): 22–43, 64–76.

Herring, Phillip F. *Joyce's "Ulysses" Notesheets in the British Museum.* Charlottesville: Univ. Press of Virginia, 1972.

Joyce, Stanislaus. *My Brother's Keeper: James Joyce's Early Years.* New York: Viking, 1969.

Kain, Richard M. *Fabulous Voyager: A Study of James Joyce's "Ulysses."* New York: Viking Press, 1966.

Kenner, Hugh. *Dublin's Joyce.* Boston: Beacon Press, 1962.

———. *Joyce's Voices.* Berkeley: Univ. of California Press, 1978.

Kreutzer, Eberhard. *Sprache und Spiel im "Ulysses" von James*

Joyce. Studien zur englischen Literatur, vol. 2. Bonn: Bouvier Verlag, 1969.

Levenston, E. A. "Narrative Technique in *Ulysses.*" *Language and Style* 5 (1972): 260–75.

Levin, Harry. *James Joyce.* New York: New Directions, 1960.

Litz, A. Walton. *The Art of James Joyce: Method and Design in "Ulysses" and "Finnegans Wake."* New York: Oxford Univ. Press, 1964.

Magalaner, Marvin, ed. *A James Joyce Miscellany: Second Series.* Carbondale: Southern Illinois University Press, 1959.

Naremore, James. "Style as Meaning in *A Portrait of the Artist.*" *James Joyce Quarterly* 4 (1967): 331–42.

Noon, William T., S.J. *Joyce and Aquinas.* New Haven: Yale Univ. Press, 1963.

O'Brien, Darcy. *The Conscience of James Joyce.* Princeton: Princeton Univ. Press, 1968.

O'Connor, Frank. "Joyce and the Dissociated Metaphor." In *The Mirror in the Roadway.* New York: Knopf, 1956.

O'Faoláin, Seán. "Style and the Limits of Speech." *Criterion* 8 (1928): 67–87.

Pound, Ezra. *Pound / Joyce: The Letters of Ezra Pound to James Joyce.* Ed. Forrest Read. New York: New Directions, 1967.

Power, Arthur. *Conversations with James Joyce.* Ed. Clive Hart. New York: Harper and Row, 1974.

Scholes, Robert. "*Ulysses*: A Structuralist Perspective." *James Joyce Quarterly* 10 (1972): 161–71.

Senn, Fritz, ed. *New Light on Joyce from the Dublin Symposium.* Bloomington: Indiana Univ. Press, 1972.

Staley, Thomas F., ed. *James Joyce Today.* Bloomington: Indiana Univ. Press, 1970.

Staley, Thomas F., and Bernard Benstock, eds. *Approaches to "Ulysses": Ten Essays.* Pittsburgh: Univ. of Pittsburgh Press, 1970.

Steinberg, Edward. *The Stream of Consciousness and Beyond in "Ulysses."* Pittsburgh: Univ. of Pittsburgh Press, 1973.

Sullivan, Kevin. *Joyce Among the Jesuits.* New York: Columbia Univ. Press, 1958.

Sultan, Stanley. *The Argument of "Ulysses."* Columbus: Ohio State Univ. Press, 1964.

Thornton, Weldon. *Allusions in "Ulysses": An Annotated List.* Chapel Hill: Univ. of North Carolina Press, 1968.

Weathers, Winston. "Joyce and the Tragedy of Language." *Forum* 4 (1964): 16–21.

Wilson, Edmund. *Axel's Castle: A Study of the Imaginative Literature of 1870–1930.* New York: Scribners, 1969.

Index

Anatomy, 99

Aristotle, 35, 89, 95, 103; Stephen's predilection for, 59, 102; and Joyce's language, 81, 83–84, 87–88, 91–92, 95–96; and grammar, 82; *Physics*, 83, 92, 176 (n. 4); *Metaphysics*, 83–85, 96, 176 (nn. 5, 8), 177 (nn. 17, 18); and discussion of Shakespeare, 85–86; and the artist, 86; *De Anima*, 92; his biological process, 139–40

Artist (artist-figure): unique configuration of syntax, 4–5; balanced structure of, 28–30; and language, 30, 33–34, 40, 86, 104, 155, 160–62; a projection of himself, 37, 41, 85, 154; and dialectic, 37–42, 152; and teaching of English, 47; and necessity of control, 47; interaction of inner world with outer world, 74–75; patterns arranged by creative mind, 97; shift from spacial to temporal progression, 98; and entelechy of language, 105; confined by patterns of language, 109, 151–52; use of order and appropriate order, 137; and meanings of the text, 150–51; "body" of, 152–54; and Joyce's own being, 154; and

syntactic devices, 158–59; circumscribed by order he uses, 161; moral pronouncements unnecessary, 167

Artist-god, 121, 159–60

Author: entity of some question, 4–6; sense of style, 28; uses of limited syntactic devices, 158; sense of authorial judgment and conviction, 162

Barnes, Djuna, 120

Barthes, Roland, 78, 174 (n. 12)

Berlitz, M. D., 47, 48, 175 (n. 5)

Biology, 65, 139–40

"Blue Book" (Wittgenstein), 25, 177 (n. 2), 178 (n. 13)

"Branching," 51–52

Bruno, 32

Budgen, Frank, 25, 29, 176 (n. 12); and artistic choice, 9; Joyce's statement on syntactic order, 47; discussion of appropriate order, 88, 175 (n. 9); Joyce's limitations as a thinker, 158

Characters: common denominator of, 3–4; distinguished from "authorial" voice, 5–6; and language, 33–36, 39–40, 71–73, 115–17, 158–59; interaction of inner world with outer world, 74–75; and de-

187

INDEX

INDEX

"Aeolus," 6, 7, 46, 50, 60, 63, 140
"Lestrygonians," 41, 46, 53, 56, 110, 117, 131–32, 171 (n. 3)
"Scylla and Charybdis," 37, 47, 63, 82, 85, 86, 90
"Wandering Rocks," 8, 45, 110
"Sirens": characteristic license and sentence order, 13, 14, 26; musical forms in, 46, 49, 62, 79, 95, 110, 115, 135
"Cyclops," 63, 118
"Nausicaa," 73, 105–6, 127, 157
"Oxen of the Sun": historical styles, 30; symbolism of foetus in, 42; various styles in, 118, 142; processes of language and life in, 149
"Circe": language as gesture in, 22–23; dramatic forms in, 46–47; refrain of 'tooraloom,' 49, 61; rhythm of Bloom's life, 59; the unconscious in, 59; special effects, 65; entelechy in, 86; disconnected words in, 118, 129; mystery of life and love, 136–37; emotion behind language, 143–45
"Eumaeus," 1, 3, 90, 118
"Ithaca": two-sided nature of language, 33; rigidity of one voice, 36; catechism of, 46; adultery in, 55, 57, 66–67, 73; sex in, 56, 66–68;

union of men, 64–65; highly patterned, 72; concept of time, 90; Bloom sinks beneath surface of words, 112–13; talking all round the important emotions, 118; infinity, 136; questions and answers in, 137–38, 151–52; intellectual search for knowledge in, 138–41
"Penelope," 35, 65
Ulysses on the Liffey (Ellmann), 32, 174 (n. 11), 177 (n. 21)

Variety: artistic, 11; of manipulated words, 16–17, 18, 29; limits and boundaries of, 128; patterned, 151–52; for characters, 152; freedom to create a language of, 160–62. *See also* freedom, license
Vico, G., 43

Weaver, Harriet Shaw, 3
Whorf, Benjamin Lee: comment on language, 31; and the English language, 47, 88–90; concept of time, 90–91
Wittgenstein, Ludwig: on language and its system, 25, 26, 173 (n. 1); artist constructs his language, 29; developing sense in sentences, 71–72; criticized universal view of philosophy, 112–13, 177 (n. 2); on calculus of language, 130, 133–34; possible uses of language, 148
Work in Progress, 22

191